Biscuit Givers

Biscuit Givers

"Everybody gets a Biscuit at my Table"

*I have been young, and now am old; yet have I not seen the righteous forsaken, nor his seed begging bread."
Ps. 37:25, KJV*

By: Dr. Barry Amacker

XULON PRESS

Xulon Press
2301 Lucien Way #415
Maitland, FL 32751
407.339.4217
www.xulonpress.com

Xulon
PRESS

© 2022 by Dr. Barry Amacker

All rights reserved solely by the author. The author guarantees all contents are original and do not infringe upon the legal rights of any other person or work. No part of this book may be reproduced in any form without the permission of the author.

Due to the changing nature of the Internet, if there are any web addresses, links, or URLs included in this manuscript, these may have been altered and may no longer be accessible. The views and opinions shared in this book belong solely to the author and do not necessarily reflect those of the publisher. The publisher therefore disclaims responsibility for the views or opinions expressed within the work.

Unless otherwise indicated, Scripture quotations taken from the King James Version (KJV) – *public domain.*

Unless otherwise indicated, Scripture quotations taken from the American Standard Version (ASV)) – *public domain*

Unless otherwise indicated, Scripture quotations taken from the Holy Bible, New International Version (NIV). Copyright © 1973, 1978, 1984, 2011 by Biblica, Inc.™. Used by permission. All rights reserved.

Unless otherwise indicated, Scripture quotations taken from the English Standard Version (ESV). Copyright © 2001 by Crossway, a publishing ministry of Good News Publishers. Used by permission. All rights reserved.

Unless otherwise indicated, Scripture quotations taken from he Holy Bible, New Living Translation (NLT). Copyright ©1996, 2004, 2007 by Tyndale House Foundation. Used by permission of Tyndale House Publishers, Inc.

Unless otherwise indicated, Scripture quotations taken from the New King James Version (NKJV). Copyright © 1982 by Thomas Nelson, Inc. Used by permission. All rights reserved.

Unless otherwise indicated, Scripture quotations taken from The Holy Bible, Berean Literal Bible (BLPH) Hispanic Version. Copyright ©2016, 2018 by Bible Hub. sed by Permission. All Rights Reserved Worldwide.

Unless otherwise indicated, Scripture quotations taken from the Amplified Bible (AMP). Copyright © 1954, 1958, 1962, 1964, 1965, 1987 by The Lockman Foundation. Used by permission. All rights reserved.

Paperback ISBN-13: 978-1-6628-5770-6
Ebook ISBN-13: 978-1-6628-5771-3

"I have been young, and now am old; yet have I not seen the righteous forsaken, nor his seed begging bread."

Ps. 37:25, KJV

DEDICATED TO:

THE THOUSANDS OF BISCUIT GIVERS
THAT INFLUENCED MY LIFE IN ANY WAY.

About the Author

Dr. Barry Amacker is a retired educator. His 50 years in education included being a band director, adjunct college professor, assistant principal, principal, assistant superintendent, and superintendent. In 2018, he was selected as the state of Mississippi's Superintendent of the Year.

In addition to his education career, Dr. Amacker served as minister of music for several churches and was a musician in the Gospel Four. He has written several songs that have been recorded by various groups.

As the author of three previous books, Dr. Amacker is a motivational speaker for schools, colleges and churches. Moreover, he has a daily radio program and a YouTube channel.

He and his wife Kathy have two children and three grandchildren. From a long list of accomplishments, he is most proud to be called "Papa Bear," by his grandchildren.

Table of Contents

INTRODUCTION xiii

Section 1 Biblical Biscuit Givers 3
    Chapter 1 God. 5
    Chapter 2 Jesus. 11
    Chapter 3 Widow of Zarephath. 15
    Chapter 4 Peter. 19
    Chapter 5 Naaman's Wife's Servant 23
    Chapter 6 Dorcas/Tabitha 27

Section 2 Twelve Baskets of Biscuits 31
    Chapter 7 Basket 1 Ourselves 33
    Chapter 8 Basket 2 Forgiveness. 41
    Chapter 9 Basket 3 Kindness 45
    Chapter 10 Basket 4 Influence. 51
    Chapter 11 Basket 5 Knowledge 59
    Chapter 12 Basket 6 Generosity 67
    Chapter 13 Basket 7 Steadfastness. 75
    Chapter 14 Basket 8 Hope 81
    Chapter 15 Basket 9 Hospitality 89
    Chapter 16 Basket 10 Encouragement 99
    Chapter 17 Basket 11 Standing in the Gap 105
    Chapter 18 Basket 12 Respect. 111
    Chapter 19 Burnt Biscuits 117

Section 3 Barriers to Biscuit Giving/Receiving. 127
    Chapter 20 Barriers to Biscuit Giving 129

Chapter 21 Barriers to Biscuit Receiving. 149

Section 4　　Setting the Table 173
　　Chapter 22 Communion. 175
　　Chapter 23 Final Invitation. 179

CONCLUSION 183
Other Books by Dr. Barry Amacker. 187

INTRODUCTION

During a trip to the city of New Orleans, Louisiana, Kathy and I visited Mother's Restaurant, a world-famous eatery in the heart of the downtown area. Our server, Pat, was very sweet and took pride in serving her tables. After bringing our meal, a few minutes later, she arrived with two wonderful biscuits along with a generous portion of butter and jelly on the side. My eyes popped out and I said, "Wow, do we get a biscuit too?" She replied, "Baby, EVERYBODY gets a biscuit at MY tables." We cut up a little bit, and the nearby tables were caught up in the moment. Before it was over, her whole area was proclaiming that EVERYBODY gets a biscuit at Pat's tables.

Later as we were driving home, I began to reflect on that encounter in the restaurant with Pat and I realized that a wonderful life lesson had been demonstrated. The lesson Pat revealed that day was that we should all be sure that everyone we encounter gets a biscuit (of sorts) from us. Of course, I am not speaking of an actual biscuit, but something uplifting that feeds the soul of individuals we come across throughout life.

As a result, the notion of Biscuit Giver had birthed in my spirit. With great excitement, I jumped in and began my research. My first question was, "Has anything previously been written about this?" Much to my dismay, I discovered that the most common definition of a biscuit giver is "one who gives yucky gifts with little or no thought to the relevance to the recipient of the gift." With such a negative connotation, my first reaction was to change my title Biscuit Giver, but instead, I decided it would be better to change the definition of a biscuit giver to a more positive view. In this book, we will have a new paradigm of biscuit giver.

New definition, **Biscuit Giver**: one who uses his or her position in life, available resources, and influence to help those around them in a positive manner.

Indeed, we should all strive to be biscuit givers. When we see people in need, we should respond. After all, God Himself goes to empty and dry places (see Isa. 58:11, ASV). Empty stomachs or situations are in need of a biscuit. This book will give examples and demonstrations of biscuit giving and receiving. My hope is that we will become more aware of helping everyone we encounter in some meaningful way as we become biscuit givers. From the earliest of ages as children, no doubt, we learned the nursery song "Patty Cake." The lyrics of this little song set the tone for enjoying baking and eating biscuits for a lifetime. The writer of this little nursery rhyme did not know Pat, though it is fitting for our purposes that it uses her name Pat (ty) in the title.

> *Patty cake, patty cake, baker's man. Bake me a cake as fast as you can. Roll it, roll it, pat it, mark it with a "B", Put it in the oven for Baby and me.*

Even as we see in the little nursery rhyme of Patty Cake, biscuit giving is a process. It says to roll it, pat it, mark it and bake it. Therefore, in developing our biscuit giving, we must

INTRODUCTION

have a giving attitude, position ourselves to give, act on the need to give, and complete the process by receiving.

Let us go! Put the biscuits in the oven and, like Pat said, "Baby, everybody gets a biscuit at my (our) table(s)!"

Section 1

Biblical Biscuit Givers

Eating, drinking, and the mention of food occur over 700 times throughout the Bible. We see eating used in dual contexts of providing for physical and spiritual necessities. In the Old Testament, there are ceremonial laws, which govern eating to enhance physical capacity as well as following the ceremonial laws. Additionally, spiritual connections are made through the reference of food and eating. In the book of John, chapter 6 verse 35 sets the table for this book beautifully, because it connects the dots between the spiritual and physical connection of food while presenting Jesus as the ultimate biscuit giver. *"And Jesus said unto them, I am the bread of life: he that cometh to me shall never hunger; and he that believeth on me shall never thirst."* (Jn. 6:35, KJV)

Section One, will present biscuit givers found in the Scriptures, and introduce you to modern-day biscuit givers who took actions in similar circumstances. In both scenarios, we will see our new definition of **biscuit givers** in action.

New Definition. **Biscuit Giver**: One who uses their position in life, available resources and influence to help those around them in a positive manner.

Chapter 1

God

> "Consider the ravens: for they neither sow nor reap; which neither have storehouse nor barn; and God feedeth them: how much more are ye better than the fowls?"
>
> Luke 12:24, KJV

The first and foremost biscuit giver is God Himself. In the beginning, God created the heavens and the earth. From the beginning of the Bible age, God set up a plan of provision. His providence demonstrates food provision for all of His animal creations and of mankind. *'Then God said, "Let the land produce vegetation: seed-bearing plants and trees on the land that bear fruit with seed in it, according to their various kinds." And it was so.'* (Gen. 1:11, NIV)

However, Satan disrupted God's original plan for our provision. In the Garden of Eden, Adam and Eve had everything they needed. When Satan, an archangel, initially rebelled against God, he was thrown out of heaven with one third of, the angels. (Rev. 12, NIV) Satan started his deceptive work there in the Garden of Eden and from that time forward, continually disrupted God's plan. God intended for all the biscuits we would ever need to be in place, but Satan, the ruler of this world, continues to disrupt the plan. The good news is that God keeps responding with a successful plan to move forward.

God's biscuit giving power is demonstrated in numerous ways based upon our needs and circumstances combined with what He is trying to accomplish. It may come as provision for our physical needs, spiritual needs, emotional needs, strong tower in the battle, protection, direction and wisdom. For examples, He provided mana for the Israelites in the desert during the 40 years following the Exodus from Egypt (see Ex. 16, NIV). He sent ravens to feed Elijah (see 1 Kings 17:2-16, NIV). Further, through His power, God gave victory in many battles throughout the ages.

One result of Satan disrupting the plan occurred when the Israelites were being held captive in Egypt, but God enlisted a biscuit giver to intervene. In the second book of the Old Testament, Exodus Chapter 3, God spoke to Moses profoundly through a burning bush and told Moses that He had seen the misery of His people and had heard their cry. God told Moses he was sending him to deliver His people from Egypt. *"So now, go. I am sending you to Pharaoh to bring my people the Israelites out of Egypt."* (Ex. 3:10, NIV)

Moses was reluctant and not feeling qualified or respected enough to do the job. He questioned God by asking, "What if they don't believe you sent me?" God told him to say "I AM has sent you." *Moses said to God, "Suppose I go to the Israelites and say to them, 'The God of your fathers has sent me to you,' and they ask me, 'What is his name?' Then what shall I tell them?" God said to Moses, "I AM WHO I AM. This is what you are to say to the Israelites: 'I AM has sent me to you.'"* (Ex. 3:13-14, NIV)

I AM is our almighty God and when He is in the house, all that He represents is covered. Here are some representations of the Great I AM.

- Jehovah Jireh, our provider
- Jehovah Nissi, our battle fighter
- Jehovah Shalom, our giver of peace
- Jehovah Raphe, our healer
- Jehovah Tsidkenu, our righteousness
- Jehovah Shammah, ever present one
- Jehovah Rohe, our Good Shepherd

Mistaken Identity

Kathy and I are huge Alabama Crimson Tide football fans. A few years back, Alabama was playing against Ohio State in the Sugar Bowl in New Orleans, Louisiana and we took the opportunity to go and spend a few days there before the game. As it turned out, we were staying in the same hotel as the Alabama team.

If you have read my previous books, you know by now, I exercise religiously every day. Much of my athletic workout clothes are Alabama Crimson Tide apparel. The first morning we were there, I went to the fitness center, wearing my Alabama apparel, and the attendant had me sign in with my name and room number. The next day I went to the fitness center, I was not wearing Alabama apparel. Besides, there was a different attendant. The new attendant said I had to pay an amenity fee to use the facility. I said, "I didn't have to pay last time, what is different?" She did not know what had happened the previous day but it occurred to me that the first day I was wearing my Alabama apparel and the attendant assumed I was part of the team. The second woman did not have that inclination. When I was viewed as an Alabama Crimson Tide team member the outcome was different from when I was not viewed as one of the team members. This was a case of mistaken identity. God sent Moses, and He is sending us with a clear identity. The great "I AM" is sending us, and we can expect the right results. When God sends us, there is no mistaken identity.

Just as God sent Moses to deliver the Israelites from slavery in Egypt, He sent Jesus to free us from the slavery of sin. God is the provider of the bread, but Jesus is the bread. He gave us Jesus as the bread of life. When He gave the Israelites manna, their physical needs were temporarily met. When He gave us Jesus, He gave us spiritual bread and everlasting life. Real bread comes from heaven and meets our spiritual needs. Jesus instructed us to pray to God for spiritual and physical needs. *"After this manner therefore pray ye: Our Father which art in heaven, Hallowed be thy name. Thy kingdom come, Thy will be done in earth, as it is in heaven. Give us this day our daily bread. And forgive us our debts, as we forgive our debtors. And lead us not into temptation, but deliver us from evil: For thine is the kingdom, and the power, and the glory, for ever. Amen."* (Matt. 6: 9-13, KJV)

The second book of Corinthians, chapter 9 declares the following: *"And God is able to bless you abundantly, so that in all things at all times, having all that you need, you will abound in every good work."* (2 Cor. 9:8, NIV)

Oh yes, God is ready to provide for all of our needs. He wants everyone to receive a biscuit at His table and abound in good works for others. God sent Jesus, and Jesus sent us to continue the process. *'And Jesus came and said to them, "All authority in heaven and on earth has been given to me. Go therefore and make disciples of all nations, baptizing them in the name of the Father and of the Son and of the Holy Spirit, teaching them to observe all that I have commanded you. And behold, I am with you always, to the end of the age."'* (Matt. 28:18-20, ESV)

Indeed, we go in "...all authority of heaven...," as said in the book of Matthew referenced above. The great I AM is sending us too. Remember all of the names of God represented in I AM and all of the blessings they cover. We are well equipped to be the biscuit givers that God intends us to be. Everybody can receive a biscuit at our table.

Chapter 2

Jesus

Then Jesus declared, "I am the bread of life. Whoever comes to me will never go hungry, and whoever believes in me will never be thirsty.
Jn. 6:35, NIV

God gave us Jesus, the bread of life to free us from sin and offer everlasting life. In His earthly ministry, He performed many miracles. Two miracles that involved bread were significant in the "everybody gets a biscuit" ministry.

Jesus Fed the Multitudes

Two of Jesus' major miracles involved God providing food, once for 5000 and a second time for 4,000. Both miracles showed the provision of the Lord. Interestingly enough, the two miracles occurred in different locations and in two different instances. Each has significance for biscuit givers.

In the first instance, recorded in Matthew chapter 14, Jesus had sought a place of solitude but the crowds followed him. He had compassion on them and ministered to them. Since it was a remote place, there was nothing to eat and they only had five loaves and two fish. Jesus takes five loaves and two fish and feeds five thousand, not including women and children and there were twelve baskets left unused. This miracle took place near Bethsaida, the northernmost tip of the Sea of Galilee in a Jewish environment.

In the second instance, recorded in Matthew 15, in a similar situation the crowds had gathered to be ministered to by Jesus. He had compassion for them because they had been there three days and there was no food. This time Jesus took seven loaves and a few small fish and fed 4,000 (plus women and children). In the end, there were seven baskets full of broken bread left over. This miracle occurred in the region of Gerasenes, in the area around the Decapolis at the southern end of the Sea of Galilee. Notably, this region was in a Gentile environment.

The significance of the two different miracles, in two different locations, demonstrates God's love and provision for both Jews and Gentiles. The inclusion of both Jews and Gentiles in these miracles indicates that God desires for "everybody to get a biscuit." While both miracles met immediate physical needs of the people, the more important point Jesus wanted the disciples to see was that He was the bread of life. Jesus said in John chapter 6, *"For my Fathers will is that everyone who looks to the Son and believes in him shall have eternal life, and I will raise them up at the last day."* (Jn. 6:40, NIV)

Chopper feeds the Men's Church Fellowship Workday

My father-in-law, Oscar Earl Stevenson, better known as "Chopper," was a biscuit giver if there ever was one. One of his most memorable biscuit giving adventures came when he cooked breakfast for the Men's Fellowship workday at Magnolia Springs Assembly of God in the city of Hurley, Mississippi. He loved to cook, and while serving in Navy, one of his duties was to cook. Therefore, he was accustomed to cooking for large groups and this breakfast should not be a big deal. Along with his famous pancakes, he was planning to cook grits. He started out with grits in the pot, but to be sure there was plenty, he added more, and more and more. Oh my, when they began to cook and swell there were grits everywhere. He filled every pot, bowl, plate, jar and any other container he could find in the church kitchen to contain the supply. Everybody got a biscuit and plenty of grits that day for breakfast. To this day, at the breakfast workdays, when Chopper's name comes up, the grits story brings laughter to the group.

Jesus Feeds the Disciples Breakfast

John chapter 21, records a time when Jesus cooked breakfast for the disciples. The disciples had been fishing all night and had not caught any fish. Jesus told them to cast their net on the other side of the boat and they caught an abundance of fish. When they came to shore, Jesus was there with breakfast cooked over a charcoal fire. Oh, yes fish and bread (biscuits).

Later, after breakfast, Jesus asked Peter three times, "Do you love me?" Each time, Peter responded, "Yes Lord, you know I love you. Jesus told Peter, "Feed my sheep." In this exchange, two things are clear to me. First, I am sure Jesus wanted Peter to be a biscuit giver. Three times, He admonished Peter to feed, and care for his sheep. Secondly, it is obvious that Jesus was a biscuit giver to Peter even though Peter had already denied Him three times, just as Jesus said he would (more about this later). Here, Jesus gives an amazing example for us to follow in our endeavors to be biscuit givers. We may have been let down and disappointed in this life, but we, like Jesus, should continue to reach out to those who have disappointed us.

Samaritan Woman

Another great example of "everybody gets a biscuit," is found in the story of the woman at the well. Jesus encountered this Samaritan woman while she was doing her daily job of drawing water at the well. The Jews despised Samaritans. Additionally, this woman was an outcast and looked down upon by her own people. Yet Jesus reached out to her and invited her to taste the good water of eternal life. *'Jesus answered, "Everyone who drinks this water will be thirsty again, but whoever drinks the water I give them will never thirst. Indeed, the water I give them will become in them a spring of water welling up to eternal life."'* (Jn. 4:13-14, NIV)

Jesus is our master example of biscuit giving and many more references will be given throughout this book. So far, we can see that his desire is for everyone to get a biscuit. In his eyes no one is too far gone, or messed up too badly. He is there when we need him, right on time. He has a purpose for all of us. He told Peter, "Feed my sheep" and he desires for us to do the same. *"For even the Son of Man did not come to be served, but to serve, and to give His life a ransom for many."* (Mark 10:45, NIV)

Chapter 3

Widow of Zarephath

'Then the word of the Lord came to him: "Go at once to Zarephath in the region of Sidon and stay there. I have directed a widow there to supply you with food."'

1 Kings 17:8-9, NIV

Chapter 17 of 1 Kings gives a "biscuit giving" account of the ages. It comes from an unlikely source through obedience and faith of a widow in Zarephath. Israel was in an extreme drought because of Israel's evil idolatry. God had first sent Elijah to a stream where God provided water and the ravens brought him food, but when the stream dried up, God sent him to a widow in the village of Zarephath.

When Elijah arrived, a widow was there gathering sticks and he asked her to bring him a little water in a jar and some bread. Being in great need herself, she replied, "...As the LORD thy God liveth, I have not a cake, but handful of meal in a barrel, and a little oil in a cruse: and, behold, I am gathering two sticks, that I may go in and dress it for me and my son, that we may eat it , and die." (1 Kings 17:12, KJV)

Even though she was expecting to eat her last meal and die, Elijah tested her faith by asking her to use her last ingredients to prepare a meal for him. He proclaimed to her, "For thus says the Lord, the God of Israel, 'The jar of flour shall not be spent, and the jug of oil shall not be empty until the day that the Lord sends rain upon the earth (Verse 14). She was obedient and acted on faith in the word of the Lord from Elijah. God fulfilled His promise for there was food for every day and the jar of flour was not used up nor did the jug of oil run dry.

The widow was the biscuit giver and Elijah was a biscuit receiver. As a result, in this situation both needs were met. The widow's supply was supernaturally extended, and Elijah was sustained as well. This act of biscuit giving led to a miracle.

We can learn from this account, we may be called upon, to biscuit give in areas that we do not feel we are equipped, but we have to jump in by faith and believe God will jump in. In order for the widow to receive her biscuit, she had to give a biscuit. Her obedience and faith released a miracle she needed.

Additionally, God reveals that his plan is for everybody to get a biscuit. The widow was an unlikely candidate for this event. When God sent Elijah to this widow, it was the first time ever that a minister of the gospel had been sent specifically to a Gentile. Not only was she a Gentile, but she was a woman. In her culture, she was not worth even noticing, and no doubt felt invisible, though God saw her and sent his most powerful minister to her.

Everybody gets a biscuit at God's table. If you feel like you are nothing, and Satan will make sure you do, remember the widow of Zarephath and know there is hope for you. You, and all of us, have a part in the biscuit giving plan.

A friend of ours gave this testimony of God's provision during a difficult time in her life.

> *"Living on Military pay in the 1960's was very difficult. I remember after putting up the Christmas tree one year we had a tough decision to make. We were faced with paying our tithes, or getting Christmas gifts for our girls. Well we paid our tithes. No one knew we were not going to have Christmas that year, but we got quite a surprise. A couple of days before Christmas a car pulled up outside of our house and the minister's wife and the Sunday school superintendent unloaded a trunk full of gifts. Additionally, we received a package of gifts from home. It turned out to be the best and most memorable Christmas ever".*
>
> *One of the children in the family added, "I remember that Christmas too. I had noticed there were no presents under the tree. I was feeling sad. I was quite surprised with all of the gifts. They were amazing, and I still have one of the dolls. I will never forget that Christmas."*
>
> *The mom ends the story by saying. "Be sure to remember our military families who are away from and have no one. I pray you will be a blessing (biscuit giver) to them the way someone blessed us."*

These examples demonstrate that God cares for us and He will provide for our needs if we will be obedient and stand on the principals of His word. Biscuit giving works! *'"give, and it will be given to you. Good measure, pressed down, shaken together, running over, will be put into your lap. For with the measure you use it will be measured back to you."'* (Luke 6:38, ESV)

Chapter 4

Peter

Then Peter said, "Silver or gold I do not have, but what I do have I give you: In the name of Jesus Christ of Nazareth, walk."

Acts 3:6, NIV

Earlier in Chapter 2, I shared the encounter Peter had with Jesus when he was asked, "Do you love me?" When Peter responded Yes, Jesus said, "Feed my Sheep." Peter did just that. Of course, we are not talking about physical food, but rather about taking care of people, we encounter.

One day Peter and John encountered a beggar at the gate to the temple courts. This man asked them for money and possibly food. However, the beggar had a bigger problem; he was crippled. 'Then Peter said, "Silver or gold I do not have, but what I do have I give you. In the name of Jesus Christ of Nazareth, walk." Taking him by the right hand, he helped him up, and instantly the man's feet and ankles became strong. He jumped to his feet and began to walk. Then he went with them into the temple courts, walking and jumping, and praising God.' (Acts 3:6-7, NIV)

Peter's biscuit giving that day resulted in a miracle. The man did not go to physical therapy, or have to re-learn to walk. No, he leaped up and ran into the temple. In fact, he caused quite a commotion. So much so, it was obvious even to their enemies that a miracle had been performed. Peter asked the crowd why they were staring at them as if they had done something. He pointed them to the power of Christ.

Peter continued to "feed my sheep," and be a biscuit giver; many people were healed in his ministry. In Acts chapter 5 we read, *"As a result, people brought the sick into the streets and laid them on beds and mats so that at least Peter's shadow might fall on some of them as he passed by. Crowds gathered also from the towns around Jerusalem bringing the sick and those tormented by evil spirits, and all of them were healed."* (Acts 5:15-16, NLT) It says, "all of them were healed." Yes indeed, everybody got a biscuit at Peter's table.

I do believe in divine healing. As a young person, I observed my Dad as a tent evangelist pray for the sick and they would recover. Mark 16 declares that those who believe will lay hands on the sick and they will recover. That practice became a basic belief in our family. As a kid, we did not have health insurance, so the trips to doctor were few, and far between. Instead of going to the doctor, we went to the altar. Let me say, I have great respect for medical professionals and the job they do. In fact, my uncle, Dr. Dempsey Amacker, was a highly respected physician in Natchez, Mississippi. Additionally, I have many friends and family members who are medical professionals. I am sure they are biscuit givers within their roles and circle of influence.

Prayer for a Student

When I was the Superintendent of Education for the Jackson County School District, attending extra-curricular activities was something I enjoyed. With six secondary schools in the district, typically, there were several activities each night. One of the most memorable moments occurred one Friday night at a high school football game.

First, let me say, it was no secret that I am a man of faith, nor did I mince words about it. On one Friday night, I was attending a high school football game and was standing on the sidelines in my usual place cheering on the team, band, cheerleaders, dance team and students; I loved my job. After a few minutes into the game, I noticed one of the football players coming towards me. When he arrived in front of me, he asked if I would pray for him. He had been injured and had to come out of the game. I felt completely honored and privileged to be asked by a student to pray for him. Well, right there on the sidelines in front of a few thousand spectators, I prayed. Before long, a couple of other people on the sidelines had joined in. Needless to say, for a few minutes we had church. Keep in mind, there are limitations to school officials' involvement with religious activity for public schools. At that moment, none of it mattered. I jumped in and gave what (biscuit) I had, and that was to help a student who had asked for prayer.

Reflecting on that night, several things come to mind. First, the student knew of my faith. Second, he felt comfortable coming over to the 'superintendent' to make his request known. Third, others around joined in. Our school district motto is "Raising the Standard" and on that night, we definitely did that. Isaiah declares the following: *"So shall they fear the name of the LORD from the west, and His glory rising of the sun. When the enemy shall come in like a flood, the Spirit of the LORD shall lift up a standard against him."* (Isa. 59:19, KJV)

Oh, by the way, the student returned to the game. The look on his face as he waved at me when he re-entered the game remains permanently seared in my mind. I would say several miracles occurred in that event.

No matter where we are, or what role we have in life, biscuit giving opportunities are there for us. We have to look for them and the miracles will follow.

Chapter 5

Naaman's Wife's Servant

'She said to her mistress, "If only my master would see the prophet who is in Samaria! He would cure him of his leprosy."'

2 Kings 5:3, NIV

Naaman's army took a young Israelite girl, not named in the Bible, forcibly from her godly home where God was honored. While in captivity, the young girl served Naaman's wife. Although she was only a maid, she did not feel unimportant to influence others. Despite the negative circumstances that led to her captivity, she had incredible faith.

Naaman was a respected commander in the Syrian army of the king of Aram, and he did not revere Jehovah God. Naaman had leprosy and through the young servant girl's contact with his wife, she was aware of this condition and wanted to help.

Because of living in a godly home, she was very aware of the prophet Elisha and his mighty miracles. The young girl spoke up and said, *"...If only my master would see the prophet who is in Samaria! He would cure him of his leprosy"'* (2 Kings 5:3, NIV). Naaman requested permission from King Ben-Hadad of Aram to go see the prophet, and it was granted. Naaman proceeded with a large gift and a letter to King Joram of Israel, who became upset and bothered by the request. Elisha heard of the King's consternation and intervened by asking that Naaman be sent to him.

When Naaman arrived, *'Elisha sent word to him saying "Go wash yourself seven times in the Jordan, and your flesh will be restored and you will be cleansed"'* (2 Kings 5:10, NIV). Naaman was disappointed in Elisha's instructions and started to go back home, but his servants spoke up and said; *"My father, if the prophet had told you to do some great thing, would you not have done it? How much more, then, when he tells you, 'Wash and be cleansed'!"'* (v.13). Naaman heeded their biscuit of encouragement, pressed on and did as the prophet instructed and he was healed!

Naaman then proclaimed, "There is no God in the entire world except in Israel, so please accept a gift from your servant." Elisha, true to the nature of God, declined to accept the gifts and chose to be a biscuit giver (more on this later).

Despite this young servant girl's negative situation, she maintained a positive attitude. With courage and incredible faith, she spoke up and shook the foundation with the events that transpired because of her actions. Her influence affected Naaman's wife, Naaman, King Ben-Hadad, King Joram, Elisha, the other servants who spoke out and everyone who is continuing to hear the story. Everybody is continuing to get a biscuit at her table.

No doubt, in her role as a maid, the young girl had the responsibility of seeing to it that her mistress was fed (hopefully some good biscuits). We can be biscuit givers in this same way if we look for opportunities beyond the normal routines of our lives. How fantastic it turned out that her biscuit giving was taken to a greater level because of her choice to speak up in faith and a miracle followed.

Aunt Maudie

Aunt Maudie, at least that is what we called her, was a God sent biscuit giver for our family. When we had our first child, we were in great need for daycare so that my wife, Kathy, could return to work. Out of the clear blue sky, we got a call from a church friend who knew a woman that would be willing to keep our son, Bradley, if we could provide transportation to and from our house. After meeting her, we knew that God had provided a wonderful blessing for our family. When Alisa, our daughter, was born 2 years later, Aunt Maudie continued to work for us. Aunt Maudie was a wonderful Christian woman who had raised 10 children of her own. When I would go to pick her up every morning she would have just finished her prayer time, and that was a good feeling knowing she would be taking care of our kids. She had a tremendous impact on our children. Her influence helped lead Brad and Alisa to continue in the ways of the Lord, particularly in the ministry of music. They both are now successful adults that make us thankful and proud.

Sometimes, Maudie would take biscuit giving to a new level. Not only did she take care of the children, but also many times she would have supper prepared when we arrived home from work; she was an excellent cook. One of our favorite dishes she prepared frequently was a big pot of turnip greens with cornbread dumplings sitting on top. It smelled delicious.

Oh my, when those dumplings soaked up some of the juice from the turnips, it was quite tasty.

She was 74 years of age at the time and never missed a day of work. She was amazing in every way. I would tease her occasionally with a wink and tell her that if anything ever happened to Kathy, I was going to ask her for a date. Believe you me, Maudie shook the foundation for our family and her memory provides a nice smell of biscuits (cornbread dumplings) cooking in the oven.

From whatever walk of life or role we play, there are opportunities to be a biscuit giver in some way. Everyone has an influence on his or her surroundings. What miracle awaits our actions?

Chapter 6

Dorcas/Tabitha

In Joppa there was a disciple named Tabitha (in Greek her name is Dorcas); she was always doing good and helping the poor.

Acts 9:36, NIV

Acts 9 records, there was a woman named Dorcas. The name Dorcas is a Greek word translated from the name Tabitha in Aramaic. Dorcas was always doing well for others. Her life was spent in service towards those who were less fortunate and she was a good example of a biscuit giver. In her ministry, she sewed clothes and gave them to the widows. She put a small needle to work with her desire to help others to be a great blessing. Her example should inspire all of us to examine what small thing we can put to good use to help others.

Once again as in other biscuit giving examples, her effort led to a miracle. Through her ministry of sewing clothes for the widows, she received a miracle in return through the widows to whom she had ministered. When she died, the women took her body, washed it, and sent for Peter who was ministering in

Lydda 17 miles away. When Peter arrived, he continued to be a biscuit giver as he prayed for her and she lived again.

Her life the second time around was even more of a biscuit giving event because many more people believed as they heard about her being raised from the dead.

Alisa's Skirt

When our daughter Alisa was about three years old, she and Kathy were looking at the big family Bible that has numerous drawings depicting significant biblical events. They came across a picture depicting scantily clad cherubs ascending in the clouds. Well, Alisa became concerned that when she went to heaven she would not be able to wear her skirt. She asked if she would be able to wear her skirt to heaven. We were taken back by the question, and did not have an answer readily available. She persisted and asked, "Can you ask Jesus if I can wear my skirt in heaven?"

Good news! I found the answer in the book of Revelation chapter 19. *"And to her was granted to be arrayed in fine linen, clean and bright, for the fine linen is the righteous acts of the saints."* (Rev. 19:8, KJV) The answer to Alisa's question is yes! You can wear your skirt in Heaven. In fact, we all will be wearing clothes sewn, not by Dorcas but us.

The word righteousness in Revelation 19:8 is "dikaiosune", which means "righteous deeds." Biscuit giving is a righteous deed and we are weaving in this life what we will wear in the next! Our wedding garments will be composed of our godly deeds according to God's metric, not man's. What will you be wearing?

Section 2

Twelve Baskets of Biscuits

~~~※~~~

"for it is God who works in you to will and to act in order to fulfill his good purpose."
                                Phil. 2:13, NIV

It is inspiring and motivating to reflect on the many contributions of people in Bible days. People of old did their part and left us good examples, but now it is our time to allow God to fulfill his good purpose through us.

As shared earlier, it is recorded in Matthew chapter 14; Jesus took five loaves and two fish and fed five thousand men (plus women and children). Everybody got a biscuit and still there were 12 baskets full that were unused. I am not sure what happened to the 12 unused baskets, but for our purposes, let us look at 12 baskets of biscuits we CAN use to continue to feed people at our table.

We will look at 12 examples of biscuit giving using our new definition. Biscuit Giver: *one who uses his or her position in life, available resources and influence to help those around them in a positive way.*

I will share scriptural examples and "real life" stories to make them relevant to us today and present biscuit givers I have known, or known of, that stepped up with a plate of biscuits in their time to fulfill God's good purpose through them.

Examples in this section will show that God uses us, and those around us, in everyday settings with ordinary people to minister to those around us from whatever role we belong. Many times, we may not be fully aware of the needs around us, but when we initiate the process, we discover there are opportunities all around us. Interestingly, when I am on the beach, sometimes I will observe seagulls flying around and if I drop one crumb of bread, I can expect a visit from them. It usually starts with just one little seagull, though once I feed one, before long I am surrounded with dozens of seagulls wanting a piece. Therefore, it is similar with biscuit giving, we must be observant, sensitive and prepared to address the needs around us. Once we jump in, everybody gets a biscuit at our table.

Chapter 7

Basket 1
Biscuit of Ourselves

"Therefore, I urge you, brothers and sisters, in view of God's mercy, to offer your bodies as a living sacrifice, holy and pleasing to God—this is your true and proper worship. Do not conform to the pattern of this world, but be transformed by the renewing of your mind. Then you will be able to test and approve what God's will is—his good, pleasing and perfect will."
Rom. 12:1-2, NIV

The first basket we have to fill, if we are going to be biscuit givers is the basket of ourselves. We have to be willing to give of ourselves in order to help others. *"For whoever would save his life will lose it, but whoever loses his life for my sake will find it."* (Matt. 16:25, ESV)

Only by giving ourselves up for others can we redeem ourselves. If we act selfishly, we shall lose ourselves altogether, but if we give ourselves away, we will strengthen ourselves. No one can give more than they can, but everyone can give themselves. We are who we are because of God and we are his to use for His glory. It is not *who* we are, but *whose* we are that compels us to give.

Moses in a Basket

When Pharaoh ordered that all of the babies in Egypt be killed, Moses' parents put him in a basket and sent him down the Nile River in order to save his life. As it turns out, Pharaoh's daughter found him and took him to raise. As a result, Moses became Pharaoh's grandson. Moses was in a position to live a life of favor, but he chose not to be a part of Pharaoh's regime. *"By faith Moses, when he had grown up, refused to be known as the son Pharaoh's daughter. He chose to be mistreated along with the people of God rather than to enjoy the fleeting pleasures of sin."* (Heb. 11:24-25, NIV)

Moses chose the difficulty that went along with being God's servant and leading the children of Israel. As the leader of the children of Israel, he gave of himself by standing in the gap on their behalf with God. He faced many enemies, hardships and trials.

Bradley in a Basket

Moses' parents put him in a basket and left him in God's hands and it worked out for all of our benefit. I want to inform you that Kathy and I put our son in a basket and left him in the hands of the Lord too.

When our son Bradley was first born, he was so small that we carried him around in a basket. Bradley was our first-born and we had to get used to the new routines of having a baby.

We were ministers of music at Calvary Assembly of God in Theodore, Alabama, at that time. I remember one Sunday night after the service; we were going about our regular routine of greeting people, putting away music, and securing equipment. Well, about half way home we realized we had left Bradley asleep in his basket on the front pew of the church where we had been sitting. Oh my goodness, we turned around and drove back to the church, as fast as we could. Our imaginations ran wild thinking about what if he woke up in the middle of the dark church, all alone. We had dedicated him to the Lord, though we did not intend to give him physically back that night.

From our experience of leaving Bradley in his basket, I can only imagine the courage it took for Moses' parents to put their son in a basket and send him down the river, but they did what they had to do to save his life. If you read the story, all was well as God provided a way for his wellbeing. Because of Moses parent's biscuit giving, many miracles were performed through Moses as he stood in the gap for a generation(s).

By the way, when we returned to the locked, dark, empty church, Brad was sound asleep in his basket. He never knew (until later in life) that we had left him.

Choosing to be in the basket to serve by helping others will lead to difficulties that we have to be prepared to face. Paul urged the brothers and sisters in Romans 12, to dedicate their lives as living sacrifices to God and to dedicate their lives to honor and bring Glory to God. This admonishment applies to us today.

Further, In Paul's final words to the elders of the church in Ephesus, he tells them that in EVERYTHING he did, the goal was to help those in need, and he reminded them of Jesus's words "It is more blessed to give than to receive." (Acts 20:35,

NIV) So, what is everything? I believe if we are going to give in everything we do, it will involve our total being, meaning our physical capacity, mental capacity, emotional capacity and spiritual capacity. It is understood, we must have something in order to give something. With that said, we must prepare ourselves and develop our capacity in a physical, mental, emotional, and spiritual manner. Our approach to development should be deliberate, intentional and routine. When we are in a prepared, synergized state physically, mentally, emotionally and spiritually, we are positioned to respond to the world around us effectively.

In my book Power to Press On (Xulon, 2012), I give a thorough presentation on specific ways to develop in each of our physical, mental, emotional, and spiritual capacities. Here is a brief overview of the concepts presented in Power to Press On.

Physical

Preparing physically should result in a fit body and can be accomplished by developing a good relationship with food through a proper diet and nutrition, exercise, and rest. It requires consistent application of activities that lead to achieving desired physical goals. Because we belong to God, there is additional responsibility to take care of our bodies. In I Corinthians 6:15-20, Paul clearly stressed that our bodies are members of Christ, and are the temple of the Holy Spirit. He declared we are bought with a price and that we should glorify God in body and spirit.

We absolutely can take control of our bodies and physical well-being. It has been said, "health- care is self-care." Medical professionals say that our body replaces 96% of its cells over a 12-month period of time. We can improve our health by making sure the replacement cells are better than the ones being replaced. I have heard it said, "If we fail to take control of our bodies, our figure 8 will turn into a figure O." We must stay fit enough to raise our hands in praise, and bend our knees in prayer.

(Note to self: A biscuit has 190 calories not including butter and jelly!)

Mental

Mental preparation should lead us to a sharp mind, which can be improved by reading, engaging in work, and stretch learning. Having a sharp mind is vitally important. Our brain is the most important organ in our body because it manages every function of our being. A good test of this point is to stand on one foot and notice how your brain works to help you maintain your balance. I observe when I do this how my ankles, feet, and legs move quickly to provide the balance needed. Now when I do this with my eyes closed, I can only last a few seconds because I have shut my brain out of the process. We must find ways to keep our mind sharp.

Emotional

No doubt being emotionally prepared is a necessity to a biscuit giver. As we try to help others in need, we have to be emotionally healthy. The last thing individuals we are trying to help need is interaction with an emotionally unstable person. Key components of maintaining emotional health are keeping a journal, filling others bucket with positive interaction, rest, relaxation, and recreation.

Spiritual

Rest assured, when we help someone from a spiritual perspective we will face the enemy. We will have to be ready. When the disciples attempted to deliver the man from demons, they were unsuccessful. When the disciples asked why they were not successful, Jesus told them it required preparation through fasting and praying. The same is true for us; Ephesians chapter 6 declares we do not wrestle with flesh and blood. *"For we wrestle not against flesh and blood, but against principalities, against powers, against the rulers of the darkness of this world, against spiritual wickedness in high places."* (Eph. 6:12, KJV)

In order to prepare spiritually, we need to take specific steps to mature in our spiritual capacity. Daily devotion, prayer, Bible reading, and fasting are great individual things we should do. Corporately, we grow as we meet and work with other believers of like faith. We can join forces as we learn together and encourage one another.

Synergetic State

When our physical, mental, emotional and spiritual dimensions are all functioning at a high level and begin to interact with each other, we are experiencing a synergetic state of being. Heart Math Institute through research has quantified the notion that when we are functioning at a high level our head, and heart brains produce an electromagnetic field that can be detected on others several feet away (more on this later). What a powerful asset this synergetic state is to a biscuit giver. After all, how will we ever be able to jump-start someone else's battery if ours is dead too. *"For we are his workmanship, created in Christ Jesus for good works, which God prepared beforehand, that we should walk in them."* (Eph. 2:10, ESV)

How can we pull a car to safety, if we are stuck? I experienced this first hand not long ago. Kathy and I were at our get-a-way river house preparing everything for a flood that was coming. We were going to move the boat, which was on a trailer, to safety on high ground. I attached the trailer to the truck and as I started to pull out, the tires on the truck started spinning. Boom, I was stuck. Not to be defeated, I proceeded to attach my other truck to the stuck truck and boat. I got in one truck, Kathy was in the other and on my signal, we both hit the gas. Nothing moved! Now I have two stuck trucks, with a stuck boat on a trailer.

By this time, it was apparent we were not prepared to deal with this situation. Although, I was reluctant to do so, Kathy called a wrecker. The guy on the wrecker was prepared, with all of the right equipment. He did not leave the solid blacktop. He stayed on the solid ground and attached a wench to the first truck. When he hit the leaver, little by little the complete train of stuck vehicles started to move. Within five minutes, we were out of there ready to roll.

If we are going to be biscuit givers, we have to arrive on the scene of need, with the right equipment and be operating on solid ground.

Ingredients Needed in the Recipe of a Biscuit of Ourselves
- Prepare yourself to be able to give to others through physical capacity.

- Prepare yourself to be able to give to others through mentally capacity.
- Prepare yourself to be able to give to others through emotional capacity.
- Prepare yourself to be able to give to others through spiritual capacity.
- Develop your synergetic state in order to recognize needs and ways to help.
- Donate Blood.
- Donate your time and resources.
- Give your time and be on time to meet with people you are helping.
- Keep your word.
- Present yourself as friendly.
- Pray with and for those in need.
- Live a life that will inspire others.

Chapter 8

Basket 2
Biscuits of Forgiveness

"And be ye kind one to another, tenderhearted, forgiving one another, even as God for Christ's sake hath forgiven you."

Eph. 4:32, KJV

Forgiveness biscuits from our basket are a key factor to the biscuit giving process. First, we have to give the biscuit of forgiveness to others before we can receive the biscuit of forgiveness from God. Often, we can hold on to wrongs of the past that will block our blessings for the future. Proverbs 17:9 speaks of this concept. "One who forgives an affront fosters friendship, but one who dwells on disputes will alienate a friend." In this life it is a given that people will let us down and disappoint us. Sometimes it is from close friends, family members and form those whom we would least expect.

To give your all (physically, mentally, emotionally, and spiritually) to someone, a project, a job, a relationship, etc. and then be betrayed is hurtful. Being a biscuit giver requires that we continue to do what is right and give our all anyway. Jesus said, do not be surprised that they hate you, because they hated me and if I am in you, they will hate you. Biscuit giving does not always lead to being loved or appreciated. Instead, it is giving out of the right motive to help and being obedient to the nudge of the Holy Spirit. Our attitude of doing everything as unto the Lord helps us set aside the hurtful results that occur when we give sacrificially, and our effort is unappreciated and abused. In due time, God will make the crooked path straight and set a table before our enemies.

> *"You have heard that it was said, 'Love your neighbor and hate your enemy.' But I tell you, love your enemies and pray for those who persecute you, that you may be children of your Father in heaven. He causes his sun to rise on the evil and the good, and sends rain on the righteous and the unrighteous. If you love those who love you, what reward will you get? Are not even the tax collectors doing that? And if you greet only your own people, what are you doing more than others? Do not even pagans do that? Be perfect, therefore, as your heavenly Father is perfect.*
>
> Matt. 5:43-48, NIV

Biscuit givers share despite the mistakes of others. Jesus, our master biscuit giver, provides examples of how this works. Two wonderful examples below, share his love and forgiveness to Peter, and Judas.

Jesus Cooks Breakfast for Peter

Earlier we saw that Jesus cooked for Peter after he messed up. At a critical moment in time, Peter denied Jesus three times. Yet we see after that incident, in John chapter 21, Jesus is reaching out to Peter with love and forgiveness as he cooks breakfast (biscuits) for him. It is after people mess up that they need an act forgiveness the most. The act of forgiveness is not the same thing as a feeling of forgiveness. We can forgive with our head brain, and heart brain, but until we use our gut brain to do a forgiving act, forgiveness is not complete.

Jesus Sops with Judas

We know the story of Judas' betrayal of Jesus, but even in this bad situation, Jesus gives an amazing example of his love and forgiveness. At the Lord's Supper, the last supper the disciples had with Jesus before His crucifixion, Jesus dipped sop with Judas. Sop is the act of taking a morsel of bread and making a sandwich (biscuit) of Matzo and Horseradish, then dipping it in Charoset. This makes for a very spicy, hot sandwich. It was customary at a banquet for individuals to seek out someone they love and sop with them. Jesus knew Judas was going to betray him, yet he sought him out to sop with him. *"Jesus answered, He it is, to whom I shall give a sop, when I have dipped it. And when he had dipped the sop, he gave it to Judas Iscariot, the son of Simon. And after the sop Satan entered into him. Then Jesus said unto him, That thou doest, do quickly."* (Jn. 16:26-27, KJV)

Oh, how marvelous to know that Jesus loves us, even when we betray Him. He desires to sop with us despite our failures.

He gave the ultimate biscuit by giving his own life that we may live. Jesus offers himself as the Bread of Life to everybody at his table.

Ingredients needed in the recipe for Biscuits of Forgiveness

- Make the conscious choice to release yourself from the burden, pain, and stress of holding on to resentment.
- Remember you are not alone in feeling hurt or betrayed.
- Have patience with the healing process.
- Do not assign blame.
- Practice makes perfect. The more you forgive, the more capable you will become to forgive.
- Empty Chair Technique- Practice with an empty chair imagining the other person is there.
- Write your struggle down in a journal.
- Forgive yourself when you mess up.
- Ask others for forgiveness from someone you have hurt or when you mess up.
- Show empathy, try to understand other factors involved in the situation.
- Remember who the enemy is. Satan uses people to work his plan, as does God.
- Remember the other person's good qualities.
- Give others the benefit of the doubt.
- It is not about being right, but about making the relationship right.
- Remember, Forgiveness is good for YOU and your health.

Chapter 9

Basket 3
Biscuits of Kindness

"Therefore, as God's chosen people, holy and dearly loved, clothe yourselves with compassion, kindness, humility, gentleness and patience. Bear with each other and forgive one another if any of you has a grievance against someone. Forgive as the Lord forgave you. And over all these virtues put on love, which binds them all together in perfect unity."

Col. 3:12-14 NIV

We are living in a world with many differing opinions, points of view and ideals. Polarizations based on these differences can lead to less interaction between people and the less interaction there is between people, the less likely relationships and friendships will be developed. Having a reliable friend adds great value to our lives. Friends can give us encouragement, confidentiality, accountability, sympathy, a helping hand, honest feedback and fellowship. All of these actions and more can be found in our basket of biscuits of kindness.

Proverbs emphasizes the value of a reliable friend and points to Jesus as our model to follow. *"One who has unreliable friends soon comes to ruin, but there is a friend who sticks closer than a brother."* (Prov. 18:24, NIV)

Jesus is called "the friend who sticks closer than a brother." He left us a model to follow for showing humility and tenderness to those around us. When we follow Jesus' model of biscuit giving, not only does it directly benefit individuals we are helping, it motivates those around us to do the same and increases the possibility for everybody to get a biscuit.

A study done by, Daniel Fessler, director of the UCLA Bedari Kindness Institute, looked at how people can be motivated to be kind simply by witnessing acts of kindness. When people see kind acts, they are inspired to replicate those acts; he refers to it as "contagious kindness."

Additionally, Dr. Kelli Harding from Columbia University examined this notion in her book "The Rabbit Effect." She says that not only does helping others benefit the recipient, but it helps the giver as well. She says, the immune system, blood pressure and life span are improved, as a result of kind acts. In addition, scientists at Purdue University found those who volunteer have relief from anxiety and depression. They found people who volunteer have lower levels of the protein CRP, which is a marker of inflammation that has been linked to everything from depression and dementia to heart disease and even cancer.

Further, a series of studies in well-known journals over the past decade have shown that kindness is, in fact, contagious. Researchers, James Fowler and Nicholas Christakis, from the University of California San Diego and Harvard University conducted an exhaustive study supporting beliefs that cooperative behavior can spread from one person to many in a ripple effect of happiness. They determined that, "Emotional states can be transferred directly from one individual to another by mimicry and 'emotional contagion.' People can 'catch' emotional states they observe in others over time frames ranging from seconds to weeks." Kindness, they observed, spread to at least three degrees of separation. Heart Math Institute has quantified that one individual's electromagnetic field can be detected on another person several feet away (More on this later). *"By this everyone will know that you are my disciples, if you love one another."* (Jn. 13:35, NIV)

Showing acts of kindness adds credibility to our testimony. Additionally, it catches on to others as we combat negative feelings and spread positive ones. A great biblical example is given when four men worked together to help a paralyzed man. I am not sure which one of the four initiated it, but it was contagious and three more joined in. Here is what happened.

Friends in Action

Mark chapter 2 recounts the story of a paralytic. In this account, four men show an act of kindness that changed everything for the man that was paralyzed. It affected others of that day and continues to influence us now as we look at this example for encouragement. These four men combined their effort physically, mentally, emotionally and spiritually in providing this act of kindness.

When Jesus was in Capernaum, he was ministering to a large crowd. In fact, it was so large that there was no room inside or outside the door. Four men arrived carrying a paralyzed man so Jesus could heal him. When the four men discovered there was no way to get inside the building, they tore off the roof and lowered him to be present with Jesus. When Jesus saw their faith, he said to them, "Son, your sins are forgiven." Then he said to the paralyzed man, "I tell you, get up, take your mat and go home. The paralyzed man did just that and everyone was amazed saying, "We have never seen anything like this.

I cannot help but connect the four friends to the four capacities of our being that need preparation in order to press on to what God has us to do. We have to be prepared physically, mentally, emotionally, and spiritually. These four biscuit givers certainly demonstrate readiness in each of those areas and are willing to use it toward this act of kindness.

First, emotional capacity is observed by their desire to help a friend in need. Additionally, they had emotional capacity to develop their own friendships in helping each other accomplish this unified goal of helping their friend.

Second, it took physical capacity to carry him. Since the venue was across town, it is likely they became tired but they pressed on. No doubt, they helped and encouraged one another along the way until they had fulfilled their objective. If they had not acted, the paralytic might still be sitting there. We have to move in one direction or the other for God to help us. God blesses our actions, but when we pray for God to help us, we need to do something. "Help us" indicates he will "help" us, not just zap the problem out of the way while we sit back and do nothing.

Third, their mental toughness came to bare when they solved the problem of not being able to get in due to the crowd. They took off the roof and used creativity to work out a system to lower the mat he was laying on into the presence of Jesus. They could have given up but they were persistent and used their self-discipline and creativity to press on.

Fourth, the demonstration of faith by the four men revealed their spiritual capacity. They knew Jesus could heal the paralyzed man and acted on their faith. Interestingly, the scripture says that Jesus saw THEIR faith (see Mark 2:5) and responded by saving and healing the paralyzed man. Sometimes we have to give a biscuit of faith to those who are so low they cannot do anything for themselves. Here again their biscuit giving resulted in a miracle.

These four guys show us how seeing the need and jumping in with all we have to help can be life changing. I hope that we too, can see the needs around us and show acts of kindness that will be contagious to those around us. If we do, research says it will be contagious and everybody will get a biscuit of kindness as our acts grow exponentially to people we do not even know. *"Bear one another's burdens, and so fulfill the law of Christ."* (Gal. 6:2, ESV)

I saw a similar situation first hand recently on a trip to Cozumel. Kathy and I had taken the ferry from Playa del Carmen over to Cozumel to tour the Island and snorkel at Sky Reef. While I was in the water, I noticed four men carrying a man in a wheelchair. The man was decked out and ready to snorkel but he could not get to the water due to the sand and rocks. Four men noticed this situation, picked up the wheelchair, carried him over to the pier and helped him get in the water. Others, including myself, observed this and joined in to help him enjoy the beautiful water and sights. The appreciation and expression that was on his face is permanently imprinted in my mind. While we were giving him a biscuit of kindness, the man in the wheel chair gave us a biscuit of appreciation with his smile.

Ingredients needed in the recipe for Biscuit of Kindness

- Acting for someone in need
- Buying a meal (biscuit) for the next person in line
- Helping an elderly person cross the street.
- Complimenting someone about their appearance
- Encouraging someone on progress on a project.
- Including people who may be alone in conversations or activities, isolation is a terrible thing.
- Volunteering at a local homeless shelter or soup kitchen.
- Spreading positivity.
- Congratulating someone who did something courageous.
- Picking up trash in public areas even if it is not yours.
- Teaching children to be kind to everyone.
- Thanking people who rarely get gratitude, like service workers and housekeeping staff.
- Letting the person with an armful of groceries go in front of you in line.
- Helping an elderly or disabled neighbor with yard work.
- Giving directions to some who is lost.
- Saying only kind words, especially on the internet.
- Lending a hand to someone in a wheelchair.
- Bringing food to a sick friend.
- Smiling, you never know whose day you will brighten with your smile.
- Visiting a nursing home and talking to the residents who do not receive visits very often.
- Holding the door for someone else.
- Being calm, even if someone is being rude.
- Not badmouthing someone, even your enemies.

Chapter 10

Basket 4
Biscuits of Influence

"Walk with the wise and become wise, for a companion of fools suffers harm."
Prov. 13:20 NIV

Steven Covey, in his book 7 Habits of Highly Effective People (New York: Free Press, 1989) indicates that all of us have a circle of influence, a circle of control, and a circle of concern. The circle of concern includes things that concern us but we cannot do anything about (i.e. weather, natural disasters, inflation, and stock market). The circle of control includes things we can do something about such as our thoughts, attitudes, decisions, behavior, and work ethic. The circle of influence, our focus here, includes the impressions we make on others, the attitudes, vibes, inspiration and motivation individuals catch from us.

People in our circle of influence may include, children, employees, coworkers, friends, relatives, and passing acquaintances. In fact, anyone with whom we are in contact, even briefly, falls within our circle of influence. Our goal should be to give a biscuit of positive influence to everyone in our circle of influence.

Children

With our own children, of course, we have the responsibility to live a Godly life before them and train them in the ways of the Lord. However, all children with whom we come in contact are watching and our actions, attitudes, and demeanor influences their lives.

We should speak a positive word over people around us, especially those over we have authority. At graduation, I always told students to "Press on!" and spoke a positive word over them during our last time together. Recently, I ran into a former student who is now graduating from college. She hugged me and said that my press on speech was all she remembered about graduation. This happens frequently and they have no idea how big of a biscuit of encouragement those words are for me.

Employees/Coworkers

Employees and coworkers can be positively influenced when we show kindness, respect, and offer them an opportunity to be heard. In a work setting, not everyone's idea will be accepted, but all ideas deserve to be heard with dignity and respect. Our influence can never be underestimated in our work setting especially if we are in a leadership position.

When the decision was made that I would not be returning as the Superintendent of Education for the Jackson County School District, I wanted to do something to preserve the spiritual influence that I had offered during the 12 years in that role. I reflected on the account of Paul in Acts 19:11, where cloths were used to take to the sick as an instrument of deliverance and healing. I purchased a couple of dozen handkerchiefs and met with various pastors in the area and together we anointed each one of them. I can honestly say, it was an especially anointed time as we prayed over the cloths. Prior to my last day, I presented each of our administrators with their own anointed prayer cloth and explained to them my hope and purpose for their use. I reminded them to rely on God's strength and to spend time in prayer with the prayer cloth. They were received with appreciation from each one. Since that time, I have seen various ones of them that have thanked me for it. In fact, I spoke to one administrator weeks later and she had the handkerchief in her pocket.

Friends

Friends already know what to expect from us. They must like us, or they would not be our friends. Fostering a positive relationship among friends is a powerful influencer in life. Not only are we influencing them, but they are influencing us. It is urgent to have quality friends in our circle.

Students' leadership influenced the future direction at St. Martin High School. I came to St. Martin High School as principal in 2000 from another district in another state. I knew no one at the school and they did not know me. The challenge for me was to bring my influence to bare at the school. My first step was to meet with the student council, introduce myself, and share my core values. Additionally, I wanted to hear from them as well. Fortunately, we bonded as our electromagnetic fields became harmonious and from that day forward, their influence permeated the environment of the school. Student influence in a school is powerful and I believe the success we had grew from that influence. Of course, the same was true with the faculty and staff and I give them a great deal of credit for our subsequent success; the rest is history. I served as a principal for five years at St. Martin High School, two years as assistant superintendent and 12 years as superintendent for the entire school district.

Relatives

Our relatives know us best and unfortunately, they may see us through eyes of too much remembrance. I am sure I am a different person now than I was while growing up. Sometimes influencing our relatives can be the most difficult, but if we consistently press on with a strong electromagnetic field that is positive, in due time, results will shine through.

Passing Casual Contacts

A passing contact with individuals, even briefly, presents an opportunity to give a biscuit of positive influence. Heart Math Institute has quantified the fact that our head and heart transmit an electromagnetic field that can be detected on other individuals 10 feet away. They have shown that one person's heart rate can be brought into a synchronized rhythm with another. They believe that through this process, a person's emotions and attitudes can be transferred to another. This is great news for a biscuit giver. It is exciting to know if I achieve a highly synergetic state through physical, mental, emotional, and spiritual preparation, individuals with whom I come in contact can be influenced in a positive way.

To demonstrate this further, there is a feat of physics called sympathetic vibrations that occurs when a note is played on one instrument; it will cause the same note to be played on another instrument. For example, if the damper sustain pedal is held down on a piano while a note is played on another instrument, that same note played by the other instrument will automatically sound on the piano. Further, the musical notes played on one instrument can cause other objects in the room to vibrate. When I am practicing my soprano sax, it can be annoying when other objects in the room begin to vibrate. However, it demonstrates the power of the influence of the musical vibrations in the room.

Our lives should be a gift of positive vibrations to people in the circle of influence. When our positive vibe strikes a chord of positivity in someone around us, then their positive chord strikes a chord of positive in others and so on everybody gets a biscuit from our influence. However, unfortunately this concept works for negative vibes as well. The choice is ours.

By the way, one day Gabriel is going to sound a trumpet and we will be called away. I definitely want the vibration of that trumpet to strike a chord in my spirit as I leave this world.

Elisha was a great prophet in the Bible days who worked under the influence of Elijah. Elisha worked hard and received as much of Elijah's influence as possible. His desire was to receive a double portion of the anointing that Elijah possessed. When Elijah was caught away, Elisha did indeed receive a double portion of God's anointing. Elisha performed twice as many miracles as did Elijah. Now when Elisha passed away, another dead man was inadvertently thrown into Elisha's grave. Elisha's magnetic field was so powerful the man came to life. What a series of biscuit of influence events we see here. Elijah gave to Elisha, Elisha influenced with his double portion, Elisha's electromagnetic field influenced after his death, and a man was raised from the dead.

If we are in a highly synergetic state through our preparation physically, mentally, emotionally, and spiritually, our very presence can influence the atmosphere in our surroundings. However, our level of synergetic state is reliant upon our effort in getting our physical, mental, emotional and spiritual capacities functioning at high levels individually, then as each highly effective capacity engages and interacts with each other, it happens.

We must give the biscuit of influence in real time, here and now. One thing about being older is that I have the opportunity to look back and see how things played out over time. Kathy and I were watching a video of our choirs from several years ago. As different individual's faces appeared on the video, we reflected on that point in time with them. However, looking back on that moment with the present knowledge in mind (many years later) of how things transpired in their lives, we realized the importance of influencing the moments in real time as they occur. With these individuals in the video, some things moved forward in positive ways, while others were unhappy, and some were even tragic. The thing is, God already knew then what the future held even though we did not. From this experience, I realized the importance of exerting my influence here and now because it could affect the future in ways we cannot imagine, but God does. *"For I know the plans I have for you," declares the Lord, "plans to prosper you and not harm you, plans to give you hope and a future."* (Jer. 29:11, NIV)

Basket 4 Biscuits of Influence

Therefore, it is safe to say that virtually everyone we contact is within our circle of influence. Through our daily and ongoing contacts, it is possible for everybody to get a biscuit at our table.

Ingredients needed in the recipe for Biscuits of Influence

- Give credit where credit is due.
- Write a reference letter.
- Speak positively about other people.
- Keep your word.
- Use your social media to give voice to the voiceless.
- Talk to people who are having a hard time socializing.
- Stick up for someone who you know has been treated wrongly.
- Take time to write a great review whenever you like the food or have received great service.
- Campaign for a cause you believe in.
- Befriend people who are considered outcasts in society.
- Promote businesses in which you have confidence.
- Be someone's exercise buddy and encourage them to press on.
- Keep a highly charged synergetic state for your electromagnetic field.
- Pay attention to individuals' electromagnetic fields around us.
- Exert your positive influence.
- Let the Holy Spirit guide, He already knows!

Chapter 11

Basket 5
Biscuits of Knowledge

"Listen to advice and accept instruction, that you may gain wisdom in the future."
                              Prov. 19:20, ESV

We have already seen that not every gift/biscuit is tangible. One of the greatest gifts one can receive is that of instruction from a wise person. Proverbs 19:20 gives us admonition regarding receiving instruction

As a beginning educator, I had a great deal to learn. I was blessed to have wonderful mentors at every level in my career (teacher, school level administrator and superintendent). I must admit sometimes the instruction was not positive, but it was exactly what I needed to hear. I am thankful for the mentors that had the courage to risk hurting my feelings and being honest with me. By receiving the correction and getting over the sting, I benefited greatly moving forward. Admittedly, there have been times, when I thought I knew better than the mentor and went my own way. Unfortunately, often I regretted not following the advice of the mentor. I am reminded of the proverbial statement, "the older I get, the smarter my parents get.

Having careers in education for nearly 50 years, Kathy and I are passionate about the process of biscuit giving in the area of sharing knowledge. Biscuit giving in the area of education can be discouraging because of the long-term feedback loop that is inherent in the process. Teachers of the primary grades may never know how their efforts benefited their young students, as they grew older. The good thing about having a long career is the opportunity to see the fruits of our labor.

Kathy is an amazing teacher, now retired, and she finished her career teaching at the high school level. Most of her career was in elementary school, but the high school experience proved rewarding because she was able to see students "walk across the stage." This experience gave her a sense of completion that was missing in the lower grades.

Over the years, she blessed hundreds of students, but here are a few tributes to Kathy from her students, in their own words.

Vanessa

(Vanessa is student who came to Kathy's class in Ocean Springs, Mississippi from the Dominican Republic. She spoke virtually no English; however, she did possess limited written communication skills. She overcame numerous, academic, social, and emotional trials to succeed in school. She graduated from high school in 2017 and is now attending college. She recently received her United States of America Citizenship after passing all of the rigorous requirements. All of us are proud of her and her family.) Here is a note to Mrs. Amacker from Vanessa.

Mrs. Amacker you are the best person ever. Thank you for all you have done for me since day one. I will always be grateful to God for giving me the opportunity to meet a human being like you. Thanks for teaching me a lot about everything and that nothing is impossible in this life no matter where I am from.

You meant the most to me in my new life in the USA because no matter how difficult it was for me, you never gave up on me until I knew that I could do more and do it better. Something that marks me the most while I was in high school is when you told me "do not worry about your Dominican accent when speaking English. The important thing is that you can communicate with people." I will never forget that.

Amy Trehern

(Amy was a third-grade student whose parents were missionaries to Africa that came back to the United States. When they returned she was behind in her academic progress and needed intervention desperately. These comments are from her parents, John and Judy Trehern.)

When we came home on furlough from Africa, we lived in Theodore, Alabama. We enrolled our daughter Amy in Nan Gray Davis Elementary school. We were happy to learn that Kathy, a longtime friend of our family, would be Amy's teacher. Because of Amy's third world circumstances and her mother's managing a missionary home with a new baby boy, Kathy discovered that Amy needed some special help to be caught up on a few points of classroom and social skills. Kathy was a

Godsend. Not only did she devote extra time but also special TLC, which helped Amy get her classwork in a life-long groove of learning.

Over the next years, Amy finished elementary, high school, and George Fox University with excellent grades. Today, she is a wonderful mother of two boys, a beloved wife, and a California State employee. The family is dedicated to Christ and is involved in several church ministries. Kathy helped immensely in establishing a passion for learning, serving, and helping others.

Luis

(Luis was a fine young man who was very capable, but needed motivation to reach his full potential. By his own admission, he had become distracted from reaching the goals needed to graduate from high school and beyond. Kathy was able to bond with him through her own positive electromagnetic field and get him on track. He graduated from Ocean Springs High School in 2018 but he still calls frequently to thank her. Luis graduated from college in 2022 and gave a commencement speech as the Student Government Association President. Here is a note from Luis.

> Good morning Mrs. Amacker.
>
> I'm currently working on my third business plan and realized how far my work has gotten me. What got me here? How did I keep moving forward? Why haven't I quit? It's because of wonderful people like you, who know that no

matter how much someone may mess up they can come out of it. I messed up horribly this semester and gave up for a while. My teachers looked at me with disappointment and I grew emotionally weak. But, I realized I have to move forward and not allow a mistake define me.

This mindset of moving forward regardless of what others think was implemented from you. You always knew I could do great things. You are one of the reasons why I will always move forward. You are the first mentor who I think of when I know I need to get up and move forward. (indeed, he did move forward and became the President of the Student Government Association of his university.)

Thank you for your teachings not only in school but in life. I love you. I hope you're enjoying retirement!!!!

These are just a few examples from hundreds of students to whom Kathy gave the biscuit of knowledge. We can see that this knowledge was more than mental, but also emotional, physical and spiritual. I know that everybody got a biscuit at her table. Not all of us may be formal teachers, but we all are in a position to offer knowledge, expertise, and wisdom to those with whom we are in contact. We may never know the impact, but the longer I am around, the clearer it becomes that giving the biscuit of knowledge matters now and in the future.

It has been said you should never tear down a fence until you talk to the person who erected it. Being able to draw from others prior knowledge of a situation is a valuable asset. There is generally more to a story than initially meets the eye.

When we go to iconic recreational theme parks with the grands and ride the thrill rides, I like to talk to someone who has already ridden the ride. I want to know the details. I typically go to the area where people are exiting the ride to see what their reaction is. There are other ways to gather this information in advance. For example, my grands go to YouTube to see the ride in action. They generally know how many drops, dips, and flips there are before we even get on the ride. Whether you talk to people, or investigate online, it is good to know, before you go.

When gathering information, it is important to consider the validity and wisdom of the source of the information. A good example is found in 1 Kings chapter 12. In this case, Rehoboam, Solomon's son, became king after Solomon passed away. The people asked Rehoboam to consider lightening the load his father Solomon had placed on them when he was king. Upon their request, Rehoboam sought counsel from the elders that had advised his father. Their advice to him was to honor the people's request and lighten their load. The advisors told him if he did so, the people would respect him and loyally follow him. Later he considered counsel from some of his own friends, who told him, now was the time to crack down on the people. After considering the two choices, he opted to follow the advice of his friends and crack down even harder than before. This decision to reject the advice of the elders, who had brilliantly advised his father, led to an eventual rebellion of the people and the short-lived kingship of Rehoboam. (see 1 Kings 12).

No doubt, as we receive knowledge or share knowledge we need to ask for wisdom. James 1:5 tells us that God will give us wisdom generously and without reproach. *"If any of you lacks wisdom, let him ask God, who gives generously to all without reproach, and it will be given him."* (James 1:5, ESV)

Ingredients needed in the recipe for
the Biscuits of Knowledge

- Pray for Wisdom
- Research
- Share your knowledge and expertise.
- Be a patient listener.
- Help someone put together a resume to find a job.
- Donate books you have already read to a public library, an orphanage, or any local charity.
- Leave a newspaper or magazine you have read in a coffee house or the bus stop so someone can read it after you.
- Tell someone the truth even if that person may not like it.
- Help a coworker who is struggling to get all their tasks done in time for the deadline.
- Build a mini public library in your yard and invite other people to come read the books or donate their used books.
- Help someone achieve a goal – as long as it will not hurt someone.

- Give others the opportunity to express their thoughts and ideas.
- Sponsor a scholarship fund for college bound students.
- Pay a student's way to Summer Camp, Band Camp, etc.

Chapter 12

Basket 6

Biscuits of Generosity

"Whoever brings blessing will be enriched, and one who waters will himself be watered."

Prov. 11:25, ESV

Giving of our resources is of vital importance throughout the world today. In a Gallop Pole of 2018 it was reported that 18 percent of respondents reported giving time to individuals, 27 percent gave money, and 48 percent helped a stranger in need. No matter where we live, or what we have, all of us can participate in the biscuit giving process by giving something. Whether we are giving actual money, in kind services, or support of any kind, giving is an important principle in the scriptures. Contributions are needed to meet the needs of the church, help the needy and provide the opportunity for God to prove himself.

Mark Chapter 12 gives the account of a widow that gave all she had, 2 mites, which is the smallest denomination of currency. This gift caught the eye of Jesus and he pointed out it was more significant than the larger gifts of the rich contributors.

> *Jesus sat down opposite the place where the offerings were put and watched the crowd putting their money into the temple treasury. Many rich people threw in large amounts. Nevertheless, a poor widow came and put in two very small copper coins, worth only a few cents. Calling his disciples to him, Jesus said, "Truly I tell you, this poor widow has put more into the treasury than all the others.*
>
> Mark 12:41-43, NIV

> *Cast your bread upon the waters, for you will find it after many days.*
>
> Eccles. 11:1, ESV

The meaning of casting your bread upon the waters is to give generously without expectation of anything in return. However, there is a promise attached to this action because it will come back to you in due time. The key to unlocking the promise is to do the deed without the expectation of anything in return, rather do it as unto the Lord and leave the results up to Him. He has promised that he will supply our need according to His riches in glory and many times, he uses us to be the supplier, other times we are the recipient from others.

Sometimes we just act by faith and obedience and let God do the rest. Kathy and I have a little get away house on the Pascagoula River and sometimes we "cast bread on the water." Yes, we will stand on our pier and throw little pieces of bread on the water. Even though we cannot see the fish, when we throw little chunks of biscuits or bread on the water, after a little while they come to the top and start smacking away. Rest assured that in our lives, there are people around us that below the surface are hurting and need a biscuit cast their way. If we will cast our bread on their water, they will be blessed. Oh, by the way, it does come back on every wave because later on when those fish grow up, we have a real good fish fry.

There are times we have to give in faith when we are not sure of what the outcome will be. This can be difficult when giving sacrificially, but If God leads us to give whatever we have to help in a situation, we must respond in faith and trust he is working his plan. We never know what one little biscuit can do to keep a person afloat to fulfill their God called purpose.

One Little Rafter

When Dad was pastoring a church in Pascagoula, Mississippi, and we were in the process of building a sanctuary, things moved along and it was a "pay as you go" project. We would raise money for this "pay as you go" project. We would do everything from having gumbo suppers for sale (with biscuits), to selling doughnuts on Saturday mornings. It was a long hard struggle and we hit one big snag. The slab was poured, the walls were up and it was time to place the rafters on the walls. The men of the church used what limited equipment that was available to them and after a whole day, only ONE rafter was in place. After that day, it was determined the men of the church did not have the capacity to do the job. Several weeks passed and as we would come to church each Sunday (we were still meeting in the tent), we would see that one rafter standing.

We began to wonder, "Will we ever get this building done?" We had no money, or equipment to proceed.

Then, one day out of the clear blue sky, Dad received a call from a man who owned a heavy equipment company. He told Dad he had been noticing that one rafter hanging there for quite a while and was wondering if he could help in any way. Of course, Dad started "having church" right there on the phone. They worked out the details, and in a few days, all 39 of the remaining rafters joined the one lone rafter on the walls. From there, the work to be done was in the scope of ability for the men of the church and they pressed on. To God Be Glory!

It is truly, amazing what God will do when we press on with our "biscuit giving" calling. Not only, does He bless us, but also our moving forward opens the door for others to biscuit give from their appropriate resources.

Backpack Buddies

Making sure students have what they need is the highest priority in schools. When students are physically present in school, providing for their needs is more possible, but during those times of the day and school year, students are not present, meeting the need is more difficult. Our staff in each attendance center is involved in a program called Backpack Buddies in which students are given food and snacks for the weekend. Food and supplies are collected through volunteers throughout the week and on Fridays and extended holidays; students are given a backpack stuffed with goodies to make sure they are fed on the weekend.

This and similar programs are great because it opens opportunities for biscuit givers to contribute, while at the same time providing for students in need.

In my home state, Mississippi, we are notorious for being generous. In fact, according to a 2014 Gallop Poll we ranked number 2 in the nation in charitable giving. When we found ourselves in need after Hurricane Katrina, we received blessings from all over the country. At the time, I was the area superintendent for one of the hardest hit communities, and we received more contributions than we could contain. Since that time, we have had the opportunity to give to surrounding states that have also experienced devastating catastrophes by responding to the need in overwhelming ways through sending supplies, and providing food and shelter for evacuees, etc. A cup that overflows with God's blessings should spill out to the world around us. As God is generous to us, he expects us to be generous to others. *"Give, and it will be given to you: good measure, pressed down, shaken together, and running over will be put into your bosom. For with the same measure that you use, it will be measured back to you."* (Luke 6:38, NKJV)

Unfortunately, not everyone responds in a positive way during a crisis. In 2020 during the coronavirus crisis, disturbing events occurred throughout the world. It was a time of chaos and confusion and an opportunity for people to show compassion and help one another. In many cases, that is exactly what occurred. However, there were other instances where people were hoarding essential items from the grocery store, leaving the shelves empty for fellow citizens. It got to the point that the governor and other community leaders made a plea for everyone to be considerate of others by purchasing only what was needed for 1 week at a time.

Like the rich fool, some store in even larger barns their treasure they cannot take with them after they die (Luke 12:8-21). They may store up "treasures for themselves," but they are not "rich toward God." *"Do not neglect to do good and to share what you have, for such sacrifices are pleasing to God."* (Heb. 13:16, ESV)

In Matthew chapter 6, Jesus says, *"Do not lay up for yourselves treasures on earth, where moth and rust destroy and where thieves break in and steal; but lay up for yourselves treasures in heaven, where neither moth nor rust destroys and where thieves do not break in and steal. For where your treasure is, there your heart will be also."* (Matt. 6:19-21, NKJV)

Good news! The spirit of biscuit giving is thriving; Gallop Poll reported in 2018 that one billion people worldwide reported having volunteered in some way during the last month. Let us keep it going! If we all cast our bread on the water, everybody will get a biscuit.

Ingredients needed in the recipe for Biscuits of Generosity

- Donate old clothes and shoes.
- Give away extra fruits and vegetables you harvested from your garden.
- Share your food with someone who cannot afford a meal.
- Give restaurant coupons and vouchers to poor and homeless people.
- Organize a garage sale and donate the proceeds to charity.
- Give the coupons you are not going to use to people who need them the most.

- Give your used but still functional luggage to foster kids. They often do not have anything to pack their clothes in when moving from one foster home to another.
- Donate old coats and blankets to local shelters.
- If you are going to a grocery store or pharmacy, check with the neighbors. If they need something, pick up too.
- Collect stuffed animals from family and friends and send them to the children's ward at your local hospital.
- Collect used baby clothes from people you know and donate them to a women's shelter.
- Donate your kid's old bikes to children who have to walk to school.
- Give out simple care packages to people you see on the street.
- Lend your tools and equipment to a neighbor who needs them.
- Donate a spare laptop to students who cannot afford one.
- Give, give, and give.

Chapter 13

Basket 7
Biscuits of Steadfastness

> *"Blessed is the man who remains steadfast under trial, for when he has stood the test he will receive the crown of life, which God has promised to those who love him."*
>
> James 1:12 ESV

Biscuit givers have to be in the right place, at the right time, with the right equipment and a good attitude, ready to fulfill their purpose. Making all of the parts of that equation work together in order to position ourselves to deliver the biscuits is quite a feat. In fact, we cannot do it on our own. We have to move and trust God through all kinds of circumstances to arrive at the right place and time for our purpose to be fulfilled perfectly.

A glaring example of God working his timing perfectly through an individual is found in the life of Joseph. He endured a lifetime of difficult circumstances ultimately to be in a position to save an entire nation. His whole life was leading him to the exact moment God needed him. Joseph was an amazing biscuit giver through his patience, persistence, preparation and pressing on.

Joseph's Journey

The story of Joseph is a vivid example of the value there is in being patient and the preparation it provides in becoming a biscuit giver in the time of need. Many things happened to Joseph during his life that prepared him for the ability to save his family and nation from a famine that ravished the region. This act of biscuit giving led to the establishment of a great nation. His life is a wonderful demonstration of the truth found in Romans 8:28 that all things work together for good to them who love God.'

Joseph was sold by his older brothers as a slave and was purchased by Potiphar, a captain of the guard of Pharaoh. Even as an indentured servant, Joseph pressed on and did what was expected of him to the best of his ability. As a result, he gained Potiphar's trust, and was given absolute control of his affairs. However, Potiphar's wife tried to seduce him into a sexual relationship but Joseph refused to participate. Potiphar's wife lied about the situation resulting in Joseph being placed in prison.

While in prison, Joseph gained the respect of the jail keeper with his work ethic and trustworthiness. Additionally, Joseph had the opportunity to please Pharaoh by interpreting dreams for him. Because Joseph found favor with Pharaoh, he was elevated into a high place of authority and power over all of Egypt.

Through a vision, Joseph received a warning of the impending famine and established a plan to save 20% of the crops for seven years. When the famine came, just as he forewarned, Egypt had plenty and was able to sell to the people throughout the region resulting in a huge accumulation of wealth. Eventually, Joseph's brothers found their way to Egypt to purchase grain resulting in reconciliation between Joseph and his family. This reconciliation resulted in Joseph's family moving to Egypt and becoming a great nation as their population grew to a multitude.

Joseph's journey reveals how God's purpose unfolds over time with circumstances, both good and bad, leading and preparing us for His perfect plan. Although it took 13 years from the time he was sold into slavery at age 17, at the age of 30, Joseph ended up in the right place at the right time, prepared and ready to deliver biscuits physically, mentally, emotionally, and spiritually.

Physically

Joseph matured over the 13 years of this journey. No doubt, there were physical difficulties he had to overcome while being left in the pit before being pulled out by Midianites merchants and sold to the Ishmaelites. Additionally, his two years in prison were most likely challenging physically.

Mentally

Joseph demonstrated himself to be "discerning and wise" Gen. 41:39. The words for *wise* and *wisdom* in the Hebrew language, (*hakham* and *hokhmah*) denote a high level of mental perceptivity. They are used in a wide range of practical skills including craftsmanship of wood, precious stones, tailoring, along with administration and legal justice. These characteristics enabled him to do the work of strategic planning and administration especially during the time of the famine. His work ethic, even in prison, led him to find great favor with the king.

Emotionally

Joseph's emotional capacity was no doubt, challenged as he dealt with being betrayed by his brothers, being lied on by Potiphar's wife and going to prison unjustly. He had a forgiving attitude that kept him in a healthy emotional state.

Spiritually

Although Joseph was a slave and unjustly put in prison, he remained faithful to the Lord and continued to live by the commandments. He learned to trust and held to the truth "I will never leave you or forsake you." God was faithful to him too, by giving him the interpretation of the dreams that gave him favor with Pharaoh. Forgiving his brothers and helping his family took spiritual depth as well. Additionally, God blessed him as he used his other skills mentioned earlier. Having a highly functioning spiritual capacity can help us do what we do, better. *"Be strong and courageous. Do not be afraid or terrified because of them, for the LORD your God goes with you; he will never leave you nor forsake you."* (Deut. 31:6, NIV)

We can take encouragement from Joseph's example by knowing, even in the bleakest circumstances, everything will work out for our good if we remain faithful. Although Joseph was a slave and wholly undeserving of this fate, he remained faithful to the Lord and pressed on. With God's help, he made something very good of his degrading circumstances and everybody got a biscuit at his table.

Ingredients needed in the recipe for Biscuits of Steadfastness

- Intercede in prayer for others.
- Intervene with resources you have.
- Be loyal.
- Be immovable during trials, and conflicts.
- Have faith.
- Be patient, waiting on God is not wasting time.
- Stay focus on the promise not the process and follow the plan.
- Read the word of God.
- Rely on friends.
- Build on a strong foundation by developing physically, mentally, emotionally, and spiritually.
- Fast and pray.
- Worship.

Chapter 14

Basket 8

Biscuits of Hope

"Hope deferred makes the heart sick, but a longing fulfilled is a tree of life."

Prov. 13:12, NIV

Giving a biscuit of hope can change, save, and direct lives in a powerful way. Each of us encounter times when we need a biscuit of hope, or need to give a biscuit of hope.

So, what is hope? Rick Snyder's, a distinguished professor of psychology at Kansas University, theory developed in the 1990s saw hope as a "cognitive process allowing individuals to plan for and execute the pursuit of goals." In other words, for hope to exist, it is essential that a person feels he or she has an ability to effectuate change and pathways to achieve that change. Wanting to accomplish something is not enough. Goals must be pursued, and a sense of progress toward reaching them is crucial.

Taking action that is driven by hope is more beneficial than just being optimistic. Optimism is a general attitude toward life that expects everything to be all right even without a specific plan. Hope, on the other hand, assumes active participation in achieving goals through planning and motivation.

In the school setting, research has shown that the best predictor of students' success is the measure of hope that they possess. In one study at the University of Kansas, they discovered how the presence of hope boosted college achievement over a 6-year period. They found that 'high-hope' students had higher GPAs, and were more likely to graduate than 'low-hope' students were. Additionally, a Gallop Poll study has found students' measure of hope is the best predictor of their success on the ACT.

Feeling hopeless at times is inevitable in this life. In today's society, there is an atmosphere of uncertainty that cannot be escaped. Here are a few things in our day-to-day life that can lead to a feeling of hopelessness.

- Fear
- Loneliness
- Depression
- An unhappy or troublesome relationship
- A burden of guilt
- Family Relationships
- Shattered dreams
- Bad habits
- Low self esteem
- Catastrophic events
- Life tragedies

Hope in God's Promises

When I am faced with what appears to be hopeless situations, I refer to the Bible. God's word is full of promises that give me hope in any circumstance I am facing. Here are a few examples that pique my interest.

> *"Blessed is the man who trusts in the LORD, And whose hope is the LORD. For he shall be like a tree planted by the waters, Which spreads out its roots by the river, And will not fear when heat comes; But its leaf will be green, And will not be anxious in the year of drought, nor will cease from yielding fruit."*
> Jer. 17:7-8, NKJV

> *"Now hope does not disappoint, because the love of God has been poured out in our hearts by the Holy Spirit who was given to us."*
> Rom. 5:5, NKJV

> *"Now may the God of hope fill you with all joy and peace in believing, that you may abound in hope by the power of the Holy Spirit."*
> Rom. 15:13, NKJV

Many examples of hope fulfilled can be found in the Bible. Presented below are several great examples of individuals who made it through difficult times.

Job

Job was sorely tried and tested; he lost everything including his children, his friends, his wealth, and his health. His wife even discouraged him and told him to curse God and die (Job 2:9). Through it all, he maintained his hope and continued to give praise to God. *"At this, Job got up and tore his robe and shaved his head. Then he fell to the ground in worship and said: "Naked I come from my mother's womb, and naked I will depart. The LORD gave and the LORD has taken away; may the name of the LORD be praised."* (Job 1:20-21, NIV)

In the end, Job was victorious and restored with a double portion above what he possessed originally. From Job we can learn to keep trusting God in hopeless situations.

The Woman with the Issue of Blood

In Luke chapter 8, there is an account of a woman who faced a hopeless situation in her physical body. Luke 8:43-38 explains that she had been sick hemorrhaging for 12 years and she had seen many physicians and was no better but rather "grew worse." As Jesus passed by, the fingers of the woman brushed the border of Christ's garment, and all at once her body felt the health of her youth return and she knew that Christ had made her whole.

As soon as the woman touched Christ's garment, He felt that "virtue had gone out of Him," and turned about and said, "Who touched me?" The disciples mildly rebuked Jesus by saying, "Thou seest the multitude thronging thee, and sayest thou, who touched me?" She must have been one of many who touched Jesus that day in the procession, but she confessed to the touching of His robe. Jesus told her, "Daughter, be of good comfort; thy faith hath saved thee; go in peace."

It is said that this woman who was healed walked with Jesus as He went to His cross, and that seeing His blood and sweat, she drew out her handkerchief and wiped His brow. It is awesome that she was there to be a biscuit giver to Jesus after he, the bread of life, had given a new life to her. Later on, as she reverently caressed the piece of linen, she found the image of the bloodstained face of Jesus imprinted on it.

This woman's plight of suffering for 12 years demonstrates that in our lives we can face hopeless situations, physically, mentally, emotionally, and spiritually for extended periods of time. She shows us that pressing on, and not losing hope is paramount if we are going to reach a positive result. Jesus, our biscuit giver, will show up at the right time and when he does, we have to be there in reach of his garment. If we give up, lose hope, and isolate ourselves, we will not be at the parade when Jesus walks by and will not receive our biscuit

Moses at the Red Sea

Pharaoh, after suffering devastating plagues and requests from Moses, made the decision to let the Hebrew people go. After the Hebrews left Egypt, he changed his mind and pursued them with his massive army. The Israelites were trapped with mountains on one side and the Red Sea in front of them. However, God had assured Moses he would receive glory over Pharaoh. Moses declared to the people, "Do not be afraid. Stand firm and you will see the deliverance the LORD will bring you today. The Egyptians you see today you will never see again. The LORD will fight for you; you need only to be still." (Exodus 14:13-14)

Then Moses stretched his hand out over the sea. The Lord caused a strong east wind to blow all night, parting the waters and turning the sea floor into dry land. During the night, the Israelites fled through the Red Sea, a wall of water to their right and to their left. The Egyptian army charged in after them. Once the Israelites were safe on the other side, God commanded Moses to stretch out his hand again. As morning returned, the sea rolled back in covering the Egyptian army, its chariots, and horses. Not one man survived!

Not only did Moses keep hope because of his faith in God, but also interestingly, when the Hebrews crossed the Red Sea they were carrying the bones of Joseph. From our look at Joseph earlier, we know that some 400 years earlier, Joseph saved the entire country. At the end of his life, he gave directions concerning not leaving his bones in exile but taking them to Israel. He wanted to dwell in the Promised Land. These directions were given from Joseph's position of faith that they would indeed, in due time, leave the land of Egypt. His belief gave hope to the people over the years (see Heb. 11:12, Gen. 50:22). God helped them conquer the land of Canaan.

Joseph's biscuit giving continued after his life ended. As is demonstrated in this example, in our biscuit giving journey, our demonstration of hope can transcend the barriers of time. People we do not even know can receive our biscuit of hope. Nevertheless, the disparagers of hope persist. It is worth noting that in 2022, Joseph's grave was vandalized amid tension and conflict in that region. The same hope that brought Joseph and the Hebrew people through their journey is still valid for us today. At times, it may seem we are surrounded with despair and are alone, but when we are walking by faith, we are not walking alone.

> *"Show me the right path, O LORD; point out the road for me to follow. Lead me by your truth and teach me, for you are the God who saves me. All day long I put my hope in you."*
> (Ps. 25:4-5, NLT)

> *"We put our hope in the LORD. He is our help and our shield. In him our hearts rejoice, for we trust in his holy name. Let your unfailing love surround us, LORD, for our hope is in you alone."*
> (Ps. 33:20-22, NLT)

Keep Holding On

There are times in our lives when we can face floods that cause us to feel hopeless. A teacher in the Jackson County School District faced a life-threatening experience during one of the most devastating disasters in United States history. In 2005, the Mississippi Gulf Coast was ravished by hurricane Katrina. Katrina approached the Mississippi Gulf Coast as a huge Category 5 system, pushing the storm surge of 28 feet and 175 miles per hour winds. As the waters began to rise, it flooded John's house and he escaped to the rooftop. Before long, the waters had overtaken the rooftop and he was swept away by the swift current. In a last gasp effort, he secured himself on a tree top limb using his belt and hung on for dear life. He prayed for God's help and NEVER lost hope. After a while, the water subsided and he was able to get out of the tree. He was found later walking down the street in a daze by the first responders.

He has shared his story many times giving biscuits of hope. Our school district moto at the time "Raising the Standard" turned out to be very fitting. Isaiah declares *"So shall they fear The name of the LORD from the west, And His glory from the rising of the sun; When the enemy comes in like a flood, the Spirit of the LORD will lift up a standard against him."* (Isa. 59:19, ESV)

From these lessons and many other Biblical examples, we can see that with God, all things are possible (see Matt. 15:26). And we too, can find strength, comfort and guidance as we act with hope in the Lord during challenging times. As biscuit givers from the basket of hope, we can share this comfort, guidance and strength with those that feel hopeless.

Ingredients needed in the recipe for Biscuits of Hope

- Show love, compassion and care.
- Make individuals feel they deserve happiness.
- Show acceptance.
- Offer help.
- Show appreciation.
- Help in individuals find their passion.
- Stay connected.
- Teach hope.
- Give words of encouragement.
- Compliment someone to increase her or his self-worth.
- Show understanding instead of passing judgment.
- Comfort someone who just lost a loved one.
- Have faith in God and His promise.

Chapter 15

Basket 9

Biscuits of Hospitality

"Contribute to the needs of the saints and seek to show hospitality."

Rom. 12:13, ESV

The notion of hospitality conjures up memories of eating and fellowship. Some of my fondest memories are of times when our family would gather for various holidays, birthdays, and other special occasions. I realize now, that the gathering did not just happen automatically, because someone (or several people) had to put it all together. Additionally, over the years I have attended many conferences and award ceremonies where banquets were held. In these cases, there was a host, a sponsor, planner and many other "biscuit givers" of hospitality.

Getting together to eat is something that is a common way of fellowship. It is amazing that my Moss Point High School graduation class of 1970 still meets for lunch once a month. It is great to see everyone and keep in touch. This is quite rare, but I give credit to our hospitality biscuit giver classmate,

Shelia Cochran Broome, who keeps it going. She makes all of the arrangements, contacts everybody and serves as our host. Unbelievably, we have around 50 attendees every month and there were over 100 classmates at our 50th class reunion.

My father in law Oscar (Chopper) Stevenson that I introduced you to earlier was a good example of a hospitality biscuit giver; he loved to help people and he was known for his cooking skills. It would not be unusual for him to invite people, he barely knew or complete strangers he saw in need, to his house for a meal. Additionally, I can remember staying with him at his river place on weekends and early in the morning, I would hear him preparing breakfast. He was famous for his pancakes. The only thing was he cooked a huge number of pancakes. He would sit a stack of about eight pancakes before me and I was thinking that was for everyone, but as it turned out, they were all for me. I ended up being a biscuit giver too, because it was not possible to eat them all by myself, I was happy to share. (Note to self, He gave a biscuit of knowledge when he told me "Barry, Remember, no matter how flat a pancake is, there are two sides to it.")

Further, the Bible places a high value on hospitality and eating, and sometimes banqueting is the focal point of that hospitality. First, when God established the specifications for the temple, the table of shewbread was a significant part of the rite. The table of Shewbread is a type of Christ and of the Lord's Supper. It points to Christ as our substance of fellowship with God that we have through His broken body and shed blood. The shewbread was always present, and was replaced every seven days with a fresh supply and the priest would eat the unused loaves. God, the ultimate biscuit giver, established a pathway for the priests to fellowship with him.

In Genesis 18:1-8, Abraham is the first person shown opening the door of his home in hospitality to others, in this case to the Lord Himself! Believers in the Bible days met together in their homes to break bread together (biscuits no doubt) and they shared freely with those in need. Jesus Himself describes the kingdom of God as a wedding banquet where the invitation has been extended to "the poor, the crippled, the lame, and the blind." Everybody gets a biscuit at His table, if they will come.

The Ark of the Covenant

Obed-edom, the Gittite, performed a unique act of hospitality that is recorded in 1 Chronicles 13. This biscuit of hospitality occurred at the request of David during his journey to escort the ark of the covenant back to Jerusalem. David, out of fear and respect for the ark of the covenant asked Obed-edom to keep it in his house. He agreed and it remained there for three months. During the three months of Obed-edom's possession of the ark, the Lord blessed him and his entire household. This ark contained the gold jar of manna, Aaron's staff that had budded, and the stone tablets on which God had written the Ten Commandments. The ark of the covenant was a symbol of faith and of God's presence. When Obed-edom welcomed the ark into his house, he was welcoming the presence of God. From this account, we can learn the importance of welcoming the presence of the Lord into our lives today. Just as God blessed Obed-edom while the ark was in his house, He blesses us when we offer hospitality to Him in our "house."

The Lord's Supper

The Lord's Supper is a famous banquet Jesus had with the disciples immediately before his betrayal and arrest. It is commemorated in various ways in various churches through communion (more on this later). Many times, during the Easter season, plays, cantatas, and musical presentations depict this famous banquet. I remember one in particular that was done at Kathy's home church, Magnolia Springs Assembly of God in Hurley, Mississippi. One year, as part of the Easter program, the church choir and drama team was doing a reenactment of the Lord's Supper. By the way, Chopper, my father in law, was a fantastic singer as well as an amazing cook. In the program, he sang "I Bowed on My Knees and Cried Holy." Since he was part of the program, he took it upon himself to cook a rotisserie chicken to be used as part of the props at the table for the Lord's Supper scene. Oh my, it smelled so good. Needless to say, when Jesus and the 12 disciples chowed down on the chicken, the script changed as they stayed on that scene a little longer than planned. Even Judas was delayed in executing his plot against Jesus. After the program, they all came back for seconds. As you can imagine, he had cooked enough to feed the multitude. I loved that guy. He was one of kind and a biscuit giver indeed.

Hospitality to a Stranger

Luke chapter 24, gives an account where Jesus had an encounter with two men while walking down the road to Emmaus. This encounter occurred after the crucifixion and the day of the resurrection. However, the men did not recognize it was Jesus. Even though they had been through so much together, they were so distraught over the events of his crucifixion, they did not recognize him. These two men opened an entire new perspective when they became biscuit givers of hospitality. When they approached the village, it appeared Jesus was going to continue on, but the two men indicated it was evening and invited Jesus to stay with them. *"As they approached the village to which they were going, Jesus continued on as if he were going farther. But they urged him strongly, "Stay with us, for it is nearly evening; the day is almost over." So he went in to stay with them"* (Luke 24:28-29, NIV)

This act of hospitality changed everything in their perception of "this man." Because of their invitation, Jesus stayed and their eyes were opened when He was at the table and broke bread with them. *"When he was at the table with them, he took bread, gave thanks, broke it and began to give it to them. Then their eyes were opened and they recognized him, and he disappeared from their sight."* (Luke 24:30-31, NIV)

So, what caused them to recognize Him? Did his sleeve fold back and expose the scars in his hands? Did they recognize his voice when He blessed the bread? Was it the touch of his strong hand as he broke the bread and gave it to them? Was it the look in his eyes? Was it an aroma of the resurrection power? While we can only speculate about the answers to these questions, we can be sure they would have missed the whole thing if they not extended hospitality to Jesus.

Regardless of what may prevent us from recognizing Jesus in our daily lives, we must offer him hospitality to walk with us, stay with us, and break bread with us in order to know him more. He is the bread of life and wants to come into our lives.

Marriage Supper of the Lamb

In his vision in Revelation 19:7–10, John saw and heard the heavenly multitudes praising God because the wedding feast of the Lamb was about to begin. The angel told John to write, "Blessed are those who are invited to the marriage supper of the Lamb" (Rev. 19:9, NIV).

This marriage supper will occur between the rapture, and the second coming. In attendance will be not only the Church as the Bride of Christ, but others as well. The Old Testament saints even though they will not have been resurrected yet, their souls/spirits will be with us in Heaven. The marriage supper of the Lamb will be a glorious celebration of all who are in Christ!

More than Food

We have to realize that hospitality goes far beyond food, banquets and celebrations. God made sure we had a place at the table through Christ Jesus. From that perspective, as biscuit givers, our role should be to do the same thing. By showing hospitality, all of our actions can ensure that others feel invited to the table both physically and spiritually.

We should not confuse assimilation with accommodation. In assimilation, the guest has to change in order to fit in appropriately. However, accommodation allows the guest to come in as they are, and we fit the setting to them. It should be noted that neither assimilation nor accommodation is bad. Both have a useful place in hospitality biscuit giving and have to be used at the appropriate times. For example, in our presentation of God's word we need to accommodate our guest with what they need to understand the message, but assimilation is required if God is allowed to make a change in their lives. The two actions work hand in hand.

Jesus invites everyone to the table. So what ways can we show hospitality that does not necessarily involve eating or celebrating? Below are some examples that come to mind.

Many churches now have second services to meet the needs of non-English speaking members. Additionally, I have seen accommodations for the hearing impaired with sign language provided.

Retired pastor friends, Keith and Gladys Kirkwood have opened a ministry to help pastors and ministers to deal with physical, mental, emotional, and spiritual challenges they face. This ministry, SafeNet, is designed to fan the flame for ministers who feel burned out and need to be refreshed physically, mentally, emotionally and spiritually.

In schools, we provide the curriculum in multiple languages. In the Jackson County School District, by utilizing online services, we are able to provide the basic curriculum in 17 languages. Additionally, we provide important information to students and parents in as many languages needed. As mentioned earlier, English as Second Language (ESL) programs are provided as well.

Schools, communities, and churches do great outreach programs to help those who are less fortunate. It has been said, "You cannot warm a person's heart, whose feet are freezing."

I can recall going on missionary trips with Dad to Mexico. We would work to help the people during the day, and have a church service at night. Dad would preach in the night service—in English! Good news! We had a translator standing beside Dad. Whatever Dad said, the translator would repeat it in Spanish. Dad typically preached a long time and these services with a translator were twice as long because we were blessed to hear it in English and Spanish. It was humorous at times to watch the translator attempt to emulate Dad's enthusiasm and energy, hand motions and all. Dad would get going and really "shuck corn" and the translator "shucked corn" right along with him—in Spanish.

An awesome act of hospitality occurs when we are able to provide the invitation to God's table to those who might not understand. *'"Then the angel said to me, "Write this: Blessed are those who are invited to the marriage supper of the Lamb!" And he added, "These are the true words of God."'* (Rev. 19:9, NIV) *'Alguien me dijo: —Escribe: "Dichosos los invitados al banquete de bodas del Cordero." Y añadió: —Palabras verdaderas de Dios son estas.'* (Apoc. 19:9, La Palabra (Hispanoamérica) (BLPH))

Consequently, the ultimate biscuit giver of hospitality has issued you an invitation. Are you coming? Will you be there? Will you accept the invitation? Will you invite others to come?

Ingredients needed in the recipe for the Biscuits of Hospitality

- Volunteer at a local homeless shelter or soup kitchen.
- Make new neighbors feel welcome.
- Bring food to a sick friend.
- Visit a nursing home and talk to residents who do not get visits from family and friends.
- Offer to babysit kids for a single parent who is struggling with work and childcare.
- Make friends with someone new to the company.
- Invite a new neighbor over for dinner or barbecue to introduce them to the community.
- Invite a neighbor or coworker who is alone for the holidays.
- Cook large portions of food and share some with your neighbors who are struggling.
- Do chores for a family member who could use some extra free time.
- Offer a ride to your neighbor who does not have a car or whose car has broken down.
- Provide roadside assistance like changing a tire or calling a towing service.
- Let a friend crash on your couch while they are looking for a new apartment
- Invite someone to church
- Invite someone to lunch after church.

Chapter 16

Basket 10
Biscuits of Encouragement

"And let us consider how we may spur one another on toward love and good deeds, not giving up meeting together, as some are in the habit of doing, but encouraging one another—and all the more as you see the Day approaching."

Heb. 10:24-25, NIV

Biscuit givers should encourage one another to press on and grow toward achieving the purpose in their lives. In these days of stress and uncertainty, everyone with whom we are in contact likely needs a biscuit of encouragement. Simple things can make all of the difference in the world. A smile, an encouraging word, an open door, a friendly conversation, a compliment, or note either written or online are just a few examples of kind encouraging gestures that lift up others. Further, as we lift up others, we feel lifted up as well, and like Pat, everybody gets a biscuit at our table.

In an effort to spice up my exercise routine, I started participating in 5k races. I have noticed that many times along the race route, spectators will give encouragement like, "You've got this," "You are doing great," "The finish line is just around the curve," or simply clap and cheer me on. That simple interaction really does motivate me. In fact, I have actually finished in first place in my age/gender category a few times and it is exciting to get a medal and the recognition for those accomplishments. As exciting as it is to receive the medals at the races, it does not compare to finishing the race of life and hearing the words "well done thy good and faithful servant."

When I am working out at the gym, I take every opportunity to encourage those around me by letting them know I have noticed their hard work. In particular, there is an older gentleman who is in the gym regularly that can barely move from one machine to the other but he presses on day after day. One day I stopped him and let him know, how inspirational his persistent effort was to me. He gave a big smile and that encouraged me. By the way, he makes sure to walk by me every day now, and I give him thumbs up! This scenario serves as a reminder to me that people want to be around those who encourage them, and avoid those negative people that tend to pull them down. In fact, when we are staying at a hotel with a room on an upper level floor, I dread hearing the voice on the elevator say, "Going down" on my way to the lobby. If I have time, I will go up first so I can start my day with someone saying, "Going up!" Oh yes, I am going up, not down.

We all need positive feedback from time to time. It may be the only metric we have to know how we are doing. Without some positive feedback, we can get discouraged by thinking there are no results from our effort. When we are doing things by faith, without a standard metric to measure results, encouragement can provide the motivation for us to press on.

A young boy, 14 years of age, responded to the nudge of the Holy Spirit to write his first song. The notion of writing a song was new to him and he lacked confidence. Because of his dyslexia, lyrics were difficult to write. One afternoon, while writing this song, he became frustrated and declared, "This is not a good song!" He balled up the paper and threw it in the trash. His twin sister, Sandra, observed what happened and retrieved the paper from the trash. As she looked over the words of the song, she realized how powerful it was. She said, "Andrae, this is good. You should continue." Well, he continued and finished the song entitled "The Blood Will Never Lose Its Power." This song and many more of his compositions blessed people across the world. Andrae Crouch became a legend in the world of gospel music. His sister's biscuit giving of encouragement resulted in many miracles as people were blessed by Andrae's music.

In my own experience in doing radio broadcasts, I have no way of knowing if anyone is listening and enjoying the programs. It means the world to me, when someone says things like, "I heard your program today and it blessed me." "I watched the YouTube episode and shared it with my friends." I am then motivated to press on.

When I was a high school principal, one of our JROTC instructors was a real encourager. He was responsible for helping hundreds of students turn the corner and find their niche in school. "Sarge," as we called him, was notorious for his greeting of "Happy Friday!" You could always count on a greeting of "Happy Friday" from him, even if it was Monday. It was amazing how much better I felt on Monday after hearing the "Happy Friday" greeting. It was a reminder that Friday was on the way. Who does not love Friday?

Oh, by the way, if you need a little biscuit of encouragement today, call 707-873-7862. There is a group of kindergartners there with an encouraging word for you.

In 1 Thessalonians chapter 4, Apostle Paul commends the readers for showing love to one another, and admonishes them to continue to lift up each other. He ends the chapter by speaking of the day when Jesus returns and tells them to encourage one another with this truth. *"Therefore, encourage one another with these words."* (1 Thess. 4:18, NIV)

As Christians, we are to encourage one another day by day, but the context of this scripture pertains to Christ's return. 'These words' referred to, speak of the day when we are caught up together to be with the Lord for eternity. This event is something we look forward to and "these words" should be the ultimate encouragement. Jesus, the bread of life, is coming for us. Oh yes, I am "Going up, not going down!"

Ingredients needed in the recipe for Biscuits of Encouragement

- Compliment someone to increase their self-worth.
- Congratulate someone when they do something courageous.
- Compliment (and even tip) the people who rarely receive gratitude like the service workers, housekeeping staff, and security personnel.
- Encourage someone who has just been through a big disappointment.
- Smile. You never know whose day you brighten with your smile.
- Send an encouraging note; to someone you know who is having a difficult time.
- Share inspiring quotes and stories on your social media accounts.
- Remember friends, family and coworkers on birthdays, and special occasions.
- Bake some cookies and leave them in the break room at work with a note of appreciation.
- Encourage yourself. Give yourself a biscuit; after all, we give the dog a biscuit when he/she does well.
- Testify of the goodness of God. Let others know about your biscuits.
- Send up the aroma of praise (biscuits smell good in the oven).
- If someone is a blessing to you, let that person know.
- Tell people you appreciate them.
- Pray for people.
- Let people know when you are praying for them.

Chapter 17

Basket 11
Biscuits of Standing in the Gap

"So I sought for a man among them who would make a wall, and stand in the gap before me on behalf of the land that I should not destroy it; but I found no one."

Ezek. 22:30, KJV

Hand in hand with encouragement, our willingness to "stand in the gap" for others is a great biscuit giving opportunity. Standing in the gap requires faith and "courage." Notably, courage is the root word of enCOURAGEment. Accomplishing good in an evil world is difficult and finding someone with courage to stand up for what is right when the going gets tough is rare.

A good biblical example that demonstrates the need and lack of courage to stand in the gap is found in Ezekiel 22. In this passage, Aaron needed someone to stand with him in repairing a breech in the wall of protection that had been destroyed, but he found no one. *"So I sought for a man among them who would make a wall, and stand in the gap before me on behalf of the land that I should not destroy it, but I found no one.."* (Ezek. 22:30, KJV)

Psalm 106:23, shows another call for standing in the gap. Verse 23 explains that God was ready to destroy the people of Israel, but because Moses stood in the gap with a petition to God, the people were spared. He "stepped between the LORD and the people"

In addition to Moses, others had the courage and insight to "stand in the gap" and intercede in times of need. In Genesis 18, Abraham interceded for Sodom. Stephen prayed for those stoning him (see Acts 7:60). Paul prayed for Israel's salvation (see Rom. 10:1). Of course, Jesus prayed from the cross, *'Jesus said, "Father, forgive them, for they do not know what they are doing." And they divided up his clothes by casting lots.'* (Luke 23:34, NIV)

In the New Testament, we are told to pray for others (see 1 Tim. 2:1). God honors prayers of people to accomplish His will and He still seeks those who will stand in the gap for friends and family, for people, groups and nations. Like Abraham and Moses, we should be willing to stand in the gap, asking God to spare and to save. *"Confess your faults one to another, and pray one for another, that ye may be healed. The effectual fervent prayer of a righteous man availeth much."* James 5:16, KJV)

When I was the superintendent of the Jackson County School District, each year, we had a mantra to bring attention to our focus for the year. One year, our mantra was "Standing in the Gap" and rather than have a guest speaker for our convocation, we invited former students back to speak and thank the teachers for standing in the gap in their lives. Over the years, we spent large sums of money bringing in guest speakers, but this convocation was the best ever. In fact, the former students received several standing ovations from the several hundred faculty members present. Here are their stories.

Student 1

Her teachers were concerned that her grades were dropping. She was not turning in her homework assignments and her attitude had changed. Some biscuit giver teachers became concerned and began to look into the situation. They discovered that her personal situation was deplorable and she had moved out of her house. She was sleeping in her car and facing several overwhelming situations. The biscuit giver teachers acted to aid. On the day she spoke at the convocation, the tears flowed down her cheek and I will never forget the simple t-shirt she wore that day was completely wet with teardrops as she told her story and thanked everyone for reaching out to her. She also announced that she had just been offered a full scholarship to Mississippi State University pursuing an engineering degree. At that point, our tears shifted to an explosion of applause and a standing ovation. The teachers had given her a biscuit of standing in the gap, but she was giving the teachers a biscuit of encouragement. It is amazing how this works.

Student 2

She came to the Jackson County School District in Third grade from a non-English speaking family. She came to the elementary school and registered herself. Over the years, her biscuit-giving teachers helped and nurtured her. Of course, she was intelligent, determined and hard working. She overcame insurmountable odds and graduated as valedictorian of her class. Amazingly, she received a full ride scholarship to Harvard University. In her valedictory address, she thanked all of her teachers, staff and most of all her parents. She noted that her parents were in the audience for the first time ever seeing her receive an award. She honored them for working so hard to provide her the opportunity to be standing there as valedictorian. As she spoke in the convocation that day, her presentation reinforced our belief that anything is possible if we do not give up. If we keep the biscuit giving mentality, eventually the biscuit will be done. Several biscuits were given out in this scenario. Can you pick them out?

Student 3

She was about to begin second grade when her father was killed in the line of duty as a first responder. Naturally, she was devastated by this tragedy in her life. During the convocation, she related how teachers reached out to her and helped her through this difficult time. She shared that the most meaningful thing she remembered was how the teachers made her feel loved and safe. She called the teachers by name, many of whom were in the audience, and expressed her love and appreciation. She was standing on the stage that day as a teacher and peer to those same teachers.

As an overcomer of this set back, she is now able to engage her students with empathy. No doubt, many students will enter her classroom with an urgent need for someone to stand in the gap.

Often, standing in the gap requires us to step into roles beyond our comfort zone and that can be scary. It is normal in our human frailty to feel inadequate when facing new challenges or during difficult situations. Honesty, I have never taken on a new job, or endeavor that I was not anxious, but God has always seen me through. Matthew 10:19 should give us comfort. *"When they deliver you over, do not be anxious how you are to speak or what you are to say, for what you are to say will be given to you in that hour."* (Matt. 10:19, ESV)

I hope that we will not be arrested for our biscuit giving, as referred to in this passage but as we face obstacles beyond the comfort zone, God will give us boldness. As Matthew 10:19 declares, God will give us the right words, at the right time, or whatever we need to respond to the need effectively.

Standing in the gap takes faith, commitment, courage and dedication. I hope we like JCSD, Abraham, Moses, Stephen, and Jesus, will give the biscuit of standing in the gap. Furthermore, like Pat make sure everybody gets a biscuit at our table.

Ingredients needed in the recipe for the
Biscuits of Standing in the Gap

- Be courageous.
- Be committed.
- Take needed action.
- Stand up for those wronged.
- Stand firm for correct, but unpopular decisions.
- Say what you mean and mean what you say.
- Be consistent with your beliefs.
- Make sure your walk is as loud as your talk.
- Develop tough skin.
- Be perceptive of needs requiring someone to stand in the gap.
- Exercise Faith.

Chapter 18

Basket 12
Biscuits of Respect

"but in your hearts honor Christ the Lord as holy, always being prepared to make a defense to anyone who asks you for a reason for the hope that is in you; yet do it with gentleness and respect,"

1 Pet. 3:15, ESV

Recognizing and respecting the value of individuals around us is a great way to be a biscuit giver. Everyone has value so, "everybody gets a biscuit at our table." 1 Timothy chapter 5 gives us a model to follow. It declares, *"Do not rebuke an older man but encourage him as you would a father, younger men as brothers, older women as mothers, younger women as sisters, in all purity."* (1 Tim. 5:1-2, ESV) In this passage, we see young, old, male, female, mothers, fathers, brothers and sisters are acknowledged. It indicates that we should show respect and not rebuke anyone.

In similar fashion, 1 Peter 5:5 instructs us to be respectful to our elders and to be humble in order to receive grace. A great opportunity to give biscuits of respect is currently presenting itself as our population ages. Census data report the number of people ages 65 and older in the United States has increased steadily during the past century, and growth has accelerated since 2011, when baby boomers first started to turn 65. Between 2020 and 2060, the number of older adults is projected to increase by 69 percent, from 56.0 million to 94.7 million. The number of people ages 85 and older is projected to nearly triple from 6.7 million in 2020 to 19.0 million by 2060. Amazingly, data regarding centenarians, people 100 years of age and up, is profound. Increasing numbers of centenarians is becoming more and more likely. An increase from around 32,000 centenarians in 1980 to more than 53,000 occurred by 2010. In 2020, the older adult population includes 92,000 centenarians, and the number could increase to nearly 600,000 by 2060. What a valuable asset the older generation is to society. Think of the collective knowledge, wisdom, information, etc. that exists within this group. *"Likewise, you who are younger, be subject to the elders. Clothe yourselves, all of you, with humility toward one another, for "God opposes the proud but gives grace to the humble."* (1 Peter 5:5, ESV)

Generational Respect

Showing respect from generation to generation has never been more critical than now. There are seven living generations in the world today. Each one has their own similarities, differences, and uniquenesses.

- The Greatest Generation (born 1901–1927)
- The Silent Generation (born 1928–1945)

- Baby Boomers (born 1946–1964)
- Generation X (born 1965–1980)
- Millennials (born 1981–1995)
- Generation Z (born 1996–2010)
- Generation Alpha (born 2011–2025)

No matter which generational category we are in, we need the biscuit of respect from each other. The biscuits may look different from generation to generation just as physical biscuits do. Within our family gatherings, there are five generations represented. Kathy and I are Baby Boomers, our son is a Generation X, our daughter is a Millennial, two of the grandchildren are Generation Z and one is Generation Alpha.

Diligent effort is required to blend all the differences into our relationships, but there is never a question about how much we love each other. A biscuit in 1901 will not be the same as 2022, though both are still biscuits and are still good.

Respect to Parents

Another biscuit of respect is that of honoring your father and mother. Scriptures are clear on this point. We should honor our father and mother, and if we do, we are promised a long, prosperous life. *"Honor your father and your mother, that your days may be long in the land that the LORD your God is giving you."* (Ex. 20:12, ESV) *"Honor your father and mother"* *(this is the first commandment with a promise), "that it may go well with you and that you may live long in the land."* (Eph. 6:2-3 ESV)

Respect to our Leaders

In the world filled with a diversity of opinions and beliefs, many times we find ourselves under leaders with whom we may disagree. Even when we disagree, which is ok, we have to show respect. We can disagree and still be Christians, and friends. *"Obey your leaders and submit to them, for they are keeping watch over your souls, as those who will have to give an account. Let them do this with joy and not with groaning, for that would be of no advantage to you."* (Heb. 13:17, ESV)

The greatest biscuit we can give our leaders is that of prayer. Though many of them we may never see or meet personally, we can pray for them from where ever we are. Biscuit givers should pray specifically for our leaders to have wisdom, guidance, protection, courage and direction in a complex world. As mentioned earlier, James declares, *"Confess your faults one to another, and pray one for another, that ye may be healed. The effectual, fervent prayers of a righteous man availeth much."* (James, 5:16, KJV) I believe everybody should get a biscuit of respect at our table, especially prayer.

Respect for All

We should show respect for everyone we encounter and begin that relationship with a clean slate. Too often, we perceive others through someone else's eyes and form wrong opinions. Moreover, it works both ways. We too, can be perceived incorrectly by misperceptions through others. As a result, we miss opportunities to work together due to a false feeling toward each other. Of course, Satan loves this division because lies and deceit are his specialty. Take time to learn individuals for yourself, and form your own opinion. *"Do nothing from rivalry or conceit, but in humility count others more significant than yourselves. Let each of you look not only to his own interests, but also to the interests of others."* (Phil. 2: 3-4, ESV)

Respect is withheld at times due to jealousy. Instead of showing respect to individuals who are excelling, they are disrespected in an attempt to discredit them. We have to remember that Satan is in the slandering business and uses good people without their knowledge. He loves to discredit us in each other's eyes in an attempt to disrupt the plan and interfere with the biscuit giving process. In fact, the person he is discrediting in our eyes may just be the person to give us the biscuit to propel us toward the miracle that awaits.

Ingredients needed in the recipe for the biscuit of Respect

- Befriend people who are considered outcasts in society.
- Give others the opportunity to express their thoughts and ideas.
- Tell someone the truth even if they may not like it.
- Do not badmouth someone, even your enemies.
- Be polite to everyone.
- Practice compassion. Put yourself in other people's shoes.
- Never make fun of someone else's misfortune.
- Give credit to where credit is due.
- Say only kind words, especially on the internet.
- Attempt to understand people or situations instead of passing judgment.

- Respect everyone's right to have their own beliefs, although we do not have to agree.
- Begin relationships with a clean slate and develop your own relationship
- Truly listen to others who are speaking to you
- Answer rudeness with kindness.
- Believe that there is goodness in everyone.
- Teach children to be kind to everyone.
- Show respect to our parents
- Show respect to our leaders
- Show respect to the environment.
- Pick up trash in public areas even if it is not yours.

Chapter 19

Basket of Burnt Biscuits

"Every man's work shall be made manifest for the day shall declare it, because it shall be revealed by fire and the fire shall try every man's work of what sort it is."

1 Cor. 3:13, KJV

"When thou passest through the waters, I will be with thee; and through the rivers, they shall not overflow thee: when thou walkest through the fire, thou shalt not be burned; neither shall the flame kindle upon thee."

Isa. 43:2, KJV

Being a biscuit giver is a delicate situation. I am not a cook, but I know that preparing a biscuit takes skill on multiple levels. There has to be a recipe to follow. You need the right ingredients blended together, in the right stages, baked for the right amount of time, and at the proper temperature. Even with the recipe being followed, each batch can be a little different. Many times, individuals have their own little "secret touch" to make it their creation. It is definitely a delicate process but no one likes a burnt biscuit as a result.

Unfortunately, in our biscuit giving process, there will be opportunities to get off track and end up burning the biscuits. Wisdom is required to maneuver through the process. Temptation, negativity, jealousy, greed, impatience, distractions, and a plethora of spiritual attacks from Satan can result in burnt biscuits.

While serving as superintendent of the Jackson County School District, I realized it takes many dedicated people to experience success. We were blessed to have many dedicated and hard-working "staffulty" (all faculty and staff) including our cafeteria staff. Biscuits are already in the oven hours before the students arrive due to the cafeteria workers early arrival and dedication.

Occasionally, I had the privilege of having a general meeting with all the cafeteria staff of the district. One year, our mantra was "Fan the Flame." The intent of the mantra was to remind us to "Fan the Flame" in each of our students as they pursued the goals for the year. In our opening meeting that year, I attempted to inspire and encourage the cafeteria staff to recognize their role in the overall success of the students. I stressed the fact that they could indeed "Fan the Flame." However, I could not resist telling them while they needed to fan the flame, PLEASE do not burn the biscuits.

Unfortunately, sometimes we just burn the biscuits. I do not know of many people who like burnt biscuits. However, there is one exception of which I know. Kathy's mom loved to burn her toast and then scrape the dark part off before eating it. The first time I observed this process, I thought it was an accident, but I learned later that she intentionally burned the toast. She liked burnt toast, plain and simple. Here are some other examples of people who chose burned biscuits.

Adam and Eve

Even though God had provided for their every need (see Gen. 3), Adam and Eve were deceived and made the decision to eat from the wrong tree, and the wrong fruit (biscuit). As a result, not only did they end up with a burnt biscuit but also everyone at their table (all of mankind) ended up with a burnt biscuit.

Israelites

When the Israelites escaped from Egypt and in the wilderness (Exodus 16), they ran out of food. God gave them a daily provision of miracle bread called mana that fell from heaven to serve as their nourishment for the day. They were instructed to get enough mana for that day only, but on the sixth day, they should collect enough for the seventh day. However, they burnt the biscuit by not following instructions. Some of the people thought it would be good to get a little extra to save for later. (You never know when you might get hungry and need a biscuit). Well, God meant what He said, and those who gathered more than the daily allotment became ill.

Esau

Esau was a descendent of Abraham, and the first born of Isaac and Rebecca, thereby was legal heir to the family birthright. However, Esau burnt the biscuits when he rejected his birthright in favor of eating a stew Jacob had prepared. By simply eating at the wrong time, Esau revealed he preferred immediate gratification of a sensual desire to patiently waiting for God to give him the birthright (more on this later). Impatience was the ingredient that burnt the biscuit. It was such a simple thing, but it produced a choice with such long-lasting and painful consequences that its effect reverberates to this day. Everybody is getting a whiff of this burnt biscuit.

Lazarus

Luke 16:19-25 declares there was a rich man who was abundantly blessed and lived in luxury every day. However, there was a beggar outside his gate that the rich man refused to help. In fact, he sent his dogs out to harm him, but instead they licked his sores. Even the dogs had pity on the beggar while the rich man did not. Here is the scriptural account.

> *"There was a rich man who was dressed in purple and fine linen and lived in luxury every day. At his gate was laid a beggar named Lazarus, covered with sores and longing to eat what fell from the rich man's table. Even the dogs came and licked his sores. "The time came when the beggar died and the angels carried him to Abraham's side. The rich man also died and was buried. In Hades, where he was in torment, he looked up and saw Abraham far away, with Lazarus by his side. So he called to him, 'Father Abraham, have pity on me and send Lazarus to dip the tip of his finger in water and cool my*

> *tongue, because I am in agony in this fire.' "But Abraham replied, 'Son, remember that in your lifetime you received your good things, while Lazarus received bad things, but now he is comforted here and you are in agony.'"*
>
> Luke 16:19-25, NIV

Several "burnt" biscuit giving points are notable here. First, we see the rich man was abundantly blessed, yet he did not use his blessed position to help the beggar. Second, both Lazarus, and the beggar die and their roles are reversed. The rich man is in hell (with burnt biscuits), and the poor man is in Heaven (with the Bread of Life). Thirdly, we see that God's eternal judgment has everything to do with how we use wealth in this life and whether we attend to those less fortunate in our midst.

It is easy to dismiss the truth of this story, by saying "I am not rich, this doesn't pertain to me." However, all of us have biscuits in our basket that can be helpful to someone. This story states it clearly. The rich man in hell wanted to warn his brothers, but the answer was "no". The brothers will have to heed the warnings given in this life. The same is true for us and here is our warning. Help those who are in need and be sure everybody gets a biscuit at your table.

Satan

A stern test of Jesus' character occurs when Satan tempts Jesus to use His powers to produce food while he was fasting.

> *"Now when the tempter came to Him, he said, 'If you are the son of God, command that these*

> *stones become bread.' But He answered and said, 'It is written, 'Man shall not live by bread alone, but by every word that proceeds from the mouth of God.'"*
>
> (Matt. 4:3-4, NKJV)

Satan is in the "burnt biscuit" business. He is out to get us to give up our birthright, just as Esau did and like he tempted Jesus to do. Satan will try to burn our biscuits through, greed, impatience, selfishness, pride, etc. When Satan tries to burn our biscuits, we can use the model Jesus imposed by relying on what "is written." Additionally, Isaiah declares we can walk through the fire and not be burned. *"When thou passest through the waters, I will be with thee; and through the rivers, they shall not overflow thee: when thou walkest through the fire, thou shalt not be burned; neither shall the flame kindle upon thee."* (Isa. 43:2, KJV)

Reality of this truth is found in the story of Shadrach, Meshach and Abednego. (These biscuits just would not burn). When Shadrach, Meshach and Abednego refused to bow down to an image of Nebuchadnezzar, he commanded they be thrown into a fiery furnace. Nebuchadnezzar was so angry he demanded that the fire be intensified seven times hotter than normal. In fact, it was so hot the guards that were tasked with throwing them into the furnace were consumed by fire (they really got burned biscuits). The account is found in Daniel, Chapter 3.

> *"And he ordered some of the mighty men of his army to bind Shadrach, Meshach, and Abednego, and to cast them into the burning*

fiery furnace. Then these men were bound in their cloaks, their tunics, their hats, and their other garments, and they were thrown into the burning fiery furnace. Because the king's order was urgent and the furnace overheated, the flame of the fire killed those men who took up Shadrach, Meshach, and Abednego. And these three men, Shadrach, Meshach, and Abednego, fell bound into the burning fiery furnace. Then King Nebuchadnezzar was astonished and rose up in haste. He declared to his counselors, "Did we not cast three men bound into the fire?" They answered and said to the king, "True, O king." He answered and said, "But I see four men unbound, walking in the midst of the fire, and they are not hurt; and the appearance of the fourth is like a son of the gods."

Dan. 3:20-25, ESV

Oh, but an amazing thing happened. Jesus joined the cookout, and they were all saved. They walked out of the furnace and did not even smell like smoke. Reassurance should rise up in us when we realize He will do the same for us and our biscuits will not burn. In fact, in the end, it is Satan that will be cast into the lake of fire for eternity and God will burn his biscuits.

Ourselves

Another burnt biscuit can occur when we allow ourselves to burn out due to our own neglect. We must stay focused and take care of the details involved in being prepared with a highly engaged and effective synergetic state. If not, we can lose our way physically, mentally, emotionally, and spiritually and end up with a basket of burnt biscuits.

When we become a biscuit giver, we have to pay attention, not get distracted and follow through. If not, we can end up with burnt biscuits. My father in law, "Chopper" as we called him was an awesome cook. As mentioned earlier, he cooked for everybody, every function, and every occasion. Consequently, when he built his workshop, he included a kitchen in the design so he could cook while he worked on projects. One day while cooking and working in the workshop, he got distracted and left the area for some reason. He completely forgot about the food cooking on the stove. He was gone for a good while and when he returned, the workshop was completely engulfed with flames. It was a total loss! The workshop was burned to the ground, tools, contents and all. Trust me the biscuits were burnt that day.

Oh, but good news! When the community and men of the church learned of this incident, they rallied together and rebuilt his barn completely. Chopper had been a biscuit giver to everyone throughout the community and they became biscuit givers for Chopper. When the guys were working on rebuilding the workshop, Chopper continued biscuit giving by cooking them lunch.

A few years later, Chopper became terminally ill. During his illness, numerous friends came to help him and when he passed away over 1000 people attended his funeral. Just as the grits over flowed everywhere at the men's prayer breakfast, Chopper's acts of kindness swelled and overflowed more than could be contained. One thing is for sure, everybody got a biscuit at Chopper's table.

To avoid having a basket of burnt biscuits we have to find the right balance between staying sharp and spiritually keen versus becoming burnt out. Just as the cafeteria workers, we have to fan the flame without burning the biscuits. *"For this reason I remind you to fan into flame the gift of God, which is in you through the laying on of my hands."* (2 Tim. 1:6, NIV)

Section 3

Barriers to Giving and Receiving Biscuits

I hope that by now, we are motivated to become a biscuit giver, but as in any new endeavor, there will be barriers to hinder us from moving forward. This section will examine some of the barriers we may face in the process of, both giving, and receiving biscuits. In 2 Corinthians, Apostle Paul presents a truth that if we sow sparingly, we will reap sparingly. Perhaps after reading this section we will recognize that the biscuit giving process is a two-way street. Yes, giving is receiving and receiving is giving. *"But this I say, He which soweth sparingly shall reap also sparingly; and he which soweth bountifully shall reap also bountifully."* (2 Cor. 9:6, KJV)

Chapter 20

Barriers to Biscuit Giving

"Each one must give as he has decided in his heart, not reluctantly or under compulsion, for God loves a cheerful giver."

2 Cor. 9:7, ESV

Indeed, there will be barriers to overcome in order to be a biscuit giver. It is one thing to want to give, but another to give. We have to come to terms with our capacity to give, desire to give and our action of giving. The scripture in 2 Corinthians 9:7 stresses we have to be a cheerful giver, not one who is compelled, or coerced into giving. When we do become biscuit givers, blessings will come. Additionally, Acts 20:35 declares it is more blessed to give than to receive. *"I have shewed you all things, how that so labouring ye ought to support the weak, and to remember the words of the Lord Jesus, how he said, It is more blessed to give than to receive.* (Acts 20:35, KJV)

What are barriers that can hinder us from being a biscuit giver? Numerous barriers to biscuit giving exist and here are a few that frequently arise.

Rejection

Fear of rejection by the person you are trying to help can be a barrier. There have been times when I felt impressed to reach out to someone for a particular need, but I hesitated for fear of it not being well received.

Recently, Kathy and I were in a restaurant and we were the only customers in the dining room. After a while, another woman came in and sat across the aisle from us. I noticed she was crying and I felt compelled to go speak to her. I hesitated and prayed in my own spirit for wisdom. I still felt I should go over and speak to her. I continued to hesitate but my heart brain would not let it go. My head brain kept talking me out of it, and therefore my gut brain was chickening out. Finally, as we were leaving, I stopped at her table and offered her encouragement for whatever the situation that was troubling her. She thanked me and said everything was fine. When we got in the car Kathy and I discussed what I did. I was not sure if I had done the right thing but I did feel good that I had reached out to her. I have experienced this type of situation many times. On some of those occasions, I would talk myself out of it and would feel terrible later on. In this case, I felt much better for having reached out, than I have felt in the past when I did not reach out.

Sometimes we are sent to be the gift for a person, organization, or community. If it is not received it can be hurtful, but Matthew 10:14 tells us to wipe the dust off our feet, press on, and leave them to their own fate. We cannot cry over spilt milk and let one rejection get us off task, leaving us with a basket of stale biscuits. *"And whosoever shall not receive you, nor hear your words, when ye depart out of that house or city, shake off the dust of your feet."* (Matt. 10:14, KJV)

In instances when we are facing rejection, it is good to try the spirit with our physical, mental, emotional, and spiritual capacity (synergetic state) and then move forward. Usually, in my experience, if I pause briefly and allow my synergetic state to come to bare and the urge is still there, I move forward. My goal is that everybody gets a biscuit at my table.

Fraud

Fraud is a big barrier to the biscuit giving process. If you are like me, the phone rings frequently throughout the day with one swindle or the other. No doubt, I may miss some legitimate requests due to an abundance of caution. Unfortunately, sometimes giving is abused when people do not use the contribution in the way it was intended. However, when I do respond, most of the time as far as I know, my contributions are legitimately used in the way it was represented. I believe that the receiver of the biscuit is the one who is responsible to do the right thing, and the giver is blessed regardless.

Friends of mine who were an awesome singing group, The Crusaders, traveled all over the country ministering with a special anointing. In their ministry a multitude of people were saved, healed, and blessed in many ways. They shared this story about how blessings can be hijacked through "biscuit takers" rather than "biscuit givers." Here is what happened in their own words.

An old tent revivalist booked us to sing for one of his crusades in California. One evening as we were singing, we noticed a woman who was sitting near the middle of the tent wearing extremely dark shades. Suddenly, in the middle of a song, she jumped up, ripped her glasses off and started screaming, "I can see! I can see!" Everyone just went wild with joy. The old evangelist jumped up, grabbed the microphone and called the woman down to interview her. Her testimony caused the crowd to erupt in rejoicing again. The evangelist went straight into receiving an offering (in big old garbage cans). He started crying and talking about "these babies all the way from Mississippi came to share God's anointing with us." They are worthy of whatever offering we can give them. Why, if I only had one biscuit, I'd give them half of it!" People were streaming forward with their offerings. At the end of the night, as we were loading the bus, he came by and handed Tim a check. Once we were on the bus and starting down the road, we were all excited to know what the offering was. Tim unfolded the check, looked at it, then handed it to me, IT WAS $25.00! Oh my, the evangelist said he would give us half of a biscuit if he had it, but I do not think he even gave half of a biscuit. I am happy to say that God supplied our need anyway according to his riches in Glory through other faithful "biscuit givers."

I try to be prudent and respond to individual's request with good judgement. If someone asks for money for a particular need, rather than give cash, I purchase whatever they have requested. For example, if they need gas money, I tell them to come over to the gas station and I will buy them gas. If they need food, I will tell them to meet me at a nearby establishment. Most times, they do not show up. One time, while implementing this process a woman who needed gas did show up and to show here sincerity, she offered to give me her puppy that was in the car. I filled her tank with gas, but did NOT take the puppy and she was in tears with appreciation. It is difficult to know when and how to respond, but with God's help we have to act in good faith. Helping those in need is not only a good thing; it is a God thing!

We have to keep in mind that what people really need is the bread of life, Jesus. When someone finds Jesus, there is no place for fraud. A great example of this is found in the account of Zacchaeus, who was a tax collector and a notorious fraudster. However, the scripture tells us "After he encounters Jesus, Zacchaeus gives half of his possessions to the poor and repays anyone he has defrauded four times as much." *"But Zacchaeus stood up and said to the Lord, "Look, Lord! Here and now I give half of my possessions to the poor, and if I have cheated anybody out of anything, I will pay back four times the amount."* (Luke 19:8, NIV) To overcome the barrier of fraud, we need to pray for wisdom, exercise prudence, and pray for those in need to meet the bread of life.

Fear of Failure

Another barrier to being a biscuit giver lies in the fear that we may not possess the necessary skills to provide the help needed. There are times when we are the only one available and we just have to jump in and do our best. It is ok if we do not perform perfectly in our attempts to help. We have to embrace our own human frailty and go for it! God will help us!!

Sometimes things do not work out as planned. What looks like a simple task to assist someone can turn out to be more difficult than initially thought. A humorous example of this concept happened when I was "helping" a little kindergarten student in the cafeteria.

As superintendent of Jackson County School District, I enjoyed being around the students and getting to know them. The principal at one of our elementary schools invited me once a month to the "Baby Bulldogs Breakfast." This was an event that involved community leaders, pastors, law enforcement, coaches, athletes, cheerleaders and anyone who serves as a good role model for the students. As I recall, the students were well trained in the cafeteria breakfast procedures. Keep in mind they were students in kindergarten through second grade. They knew to raise their hand if they needed help with getting started with their breakfast. One kindergartener held up his milk indicating he needed help opening the bottle. I stepped over to assist him (I've got this, how hard can it be) Well, I twisted, turned, grabbed, shook, pinched, grunted, and groaned but I could not open the bottle. After seven attempts, I remembered the scripture in Proverbs 24:16 that says, "A righteous man falls seven times and rises again..." The little student was waiting patiently but after a bit, he looked up at me with an expression of, like really? Then he looked over to his teacher, and back to me; still no luck. Then one of the other kindergarten students took the bottle of milk and opened it right up. By that time, everyone, including me, was amused. Most importantly, the student got what he needed and continued with his breakfast. The student knew I was trying to help and my intentions were good. We were good 'buds" from that day forward; however, I do not recall him asking me to open his milk again.

When faced with the possibility of failure while biscuit giving, we have assurance we are doing what pleases God. Finally, if we keep love as our motivation, we will likely overcome fear of failure because love NEVER fails.

Cultural Differences

Inherently we have an initial resistance to things that are different, from which we are accustomed. Unfortunately, there are those who hang on to that resistance rather than move forward, resulting in missed opportunities to be a biscuit giver. As we live the life God has laid before us, we will encounter people, places, and things that are different from us. Remember, God made it all and it is not going to change. In Revelation, John describes a scene where he saw in heaven people of all nations, kindreds, and tongues. *"After this I beheld, and, lo, a great multitude, which no man could number, of all nations, and kindreds, and people, and tongues, stood before the throne, and before the Lamb, clothed with white robes, and palms in their hands;" (*Rev. 7:9,.KJV)

My take on this passage is that if you are white on earth, you will be white in Heaven. If you are black on earth, you will black in Heaven. If you are red, brown, yellow, black or white on earth, you will be the same in heaven. Whatever nationality you are on earth, you will be that nationality in Heaven. I remember learning the little song in children's church that said, "Jesus loves the little children of the world. Red, brown, yellow, black and white they are precious in His sight. Jesus loves the little children of the world."

All of us, whether we realize it or not, are tempted at times to turn people away that we do not relate to, or if they are different. Even Jesus, in Matthew 15:21-28, did not initially respond favorably to the woman requesting deliverance for her daughter. Initially, Jesus wanted nothing to do with her.

"Then Jesus went thence, and departed into the coasts of Tyre and Sidon. And, behold, a woman of Canaan came out of the same coasts, and cried unto him, saying, Have mercy on me, O Lord, thou son of David; my daughter is grievously vexed with a devil. But he answered her not a word. And his disciples came and besought him, saying, Send her away; for she crieth after us. But he answered and said, I am not sent but unto the lost sheep of the house of Israel. Then came she and worshipped him, saying, Lord, help me. But he answered and said, It is not meet to take the children's bread, and to cast it to dogs. And she said, Truth, Lord: yet the dogs eat of the crumbs which fall from their masters' table. Then Jesus answered and said unto her, O woman, great is thy faith: be it unto thee even as thou wilt. And her daughter was made whole from that very hour.

Matt. 15:21-28, KJV

Jesus was reluctant to speak to the woman at first because she was a Canaanite, Israel's enemies from 800 years earlier. He actually put her in the same category as a dog but she was persistent in her request. Her famous words, "Yes, Lord but even the dogs eat crumbs that fall from the master's table" influenced the course of history. Her persistence and courage to disagree and challenge him brought a positive result. Jesus recognized her faith and her daughter was made whole that very hour.

This encounter was Jesus' first time to minister to a Gentile. He experienced growing pains in his own ministry when she had the audacity to disagree and challenge Him with her persistence. This was a significant event in the ministry of Jesus. He, just as we do, had to resist the temptation to hang on to previous notions and move forward with His biscuit giving. Further, the woman was a biscuit giver too because she gave all of the gentiles a biscuit with her courage that helped Jesus cross the cultural barrier and ensure that everybody gets a biscuit.

This notion may sting a little (it does for me), though the scripture tells us that Jesus was tempted in all the things that we would be tempted and He overcame. This is a great example for us to overcome the temptation to resist those who are different from us. *"For we do not have a High Priest who cannot be touched with the feelings of our infirmities, but was in all points tempted as we are, yet without sin."* (Heb. 4:15, NIV) We can learn from Jesus' model here and extend God's grace to those that are different from us, those we may not like and tend to ignore.

In addition to the spiritual need to reach across cultural barriers, other barriers hinder this process. We may want to serve someone, but other practical factors hinder us. Communication, for example, can be a huge barrier that causes frustration to set in. As mentioned earlier, it was an enriching time for our family when Kathy taught the English as Second Language (ESL) students at Ocean Springs High School the last five years of her career. She was able to help them in many ways and as we observed them in their development, they blessed us. Even though Kathy has now retired and the students have graduated, she still hears from them occasionally.

They all say the same thing, "I would not have made it without you, Mrs. Amacker."

Learning Spanish is one of my stretch learning activities in the Power to Press On plan. I have been having fun learning to speak a new language. I was excited recently when we were able to take a trip to Playa del Carmen, Mexico, for several days at an "all inclusive" resort. I must say our stay was amazing and the people went out of their way to spoil us. Additionally, it was fun for me to practice speaking Spanish. Even though most of the locals spoke English, they appreciated the fact that I was attempting to communicate in Spanish. Once they realized I was a novice Spanish-speaker, they would work with me by speaking slower, and being patient with my responses. We developed a good relationship and at times, we would "cut up" a little bit through the process. As we were departing, a few of the servers said good-bye and told me I did a good job speaking "Spanglish" (half English and half Spanish). I said, "Gracias, ya'll."

Sometimes, however, it does not work out. On one of our frequent trips to New Orleans, as always, we stopped by the Café' Du Monde to purchase an order of their famous beignets. While we were standing in line, the customer in line ahead of us was placing his order and I observed it was taking a long time. I started paying attention to what was causing the delay. As it turned out, that day the restaurant was running a special that involved getting a discounted price for their t-shirts with an order of beignets. I observed the customer was a very limited English-speaking individual and the server was having a difficult time communicating with him. Additionally, I observed that he was requesting a medium size t-shirt, but the server was telling him they were "out of medium sizes." She explained multiple times. "We have sizes in extra-large, large, and small, but NO medium t-shirts." Every time she said medium he would respond, "Ah yes, medium good?" She said, "We do not have medium." This went on and on and finally, she gave him a t-shirt (not sure, what size, but it was NOT a medium). The server was very frustrated by the time it was my turn to order. She said, "Sir may I take your order?" Well, my mischievousness popped out and I could not resist. I said, "Yes, I would like an order of beignets and a MEDIUM t-shirt. She looked at me very stodgily and said. "Don't even start with me." I let her off the hook quickly, for both of our benefits and told her I was only kidding. Our laughter broke the tension and I gladly took a small t-shirt with my order of beignets.

But, one thing is for sure, when we all get to Heaven and people from all nations, kindred's, people, and tongues, stand before the throne, and before the Lamb, we will be clothed with white robes. They will be just the right size.

Criticized

Reluctance to be a biscuit giver can occur at times due to criticism that can arise. In fact, it is likely we will be criticized if we reach out to certain people or groups of people that are not considered "good" people. A good example of this is found when Jesus had lunch with Levi.

> *"After this, Jesus went out and saw a tax collector by the name of Levi sitting at his tax booth. "Follow me," Jesus said to him, and Levi got up, left everything and followed him. Then Levi held a great banquet for Jesus at his house,*

> *and a large crowd of tax collectors and others were eating with them. But the Pharisees and the teachers of the law who belonged to their sect complained to his disciples, "Why do you eat and drink with tax collectors and sinners?" Jesus answered them, "It is not the healthy who need a doctor, but the sick. I have not come to call the righteous, but sinners to repentance."*
>
> Luke 5:22-27, NIV

Levi was a bad person in the eyes of the Pharisees and teachers of the law. They criticized Jesus for having lunch with him and other "bad" people and caused quite a stir in the community. Jesus set them straight by refocusing his mission of calling sinners to repentance. Too often, people are so busy making *rules*; they fail to listen to the *ruler.*

Jesus called Levi to follow him, and he did. We now know Levi as Matthew the disciple. We never know how ministering to "bad" people can influence the future. So, who is getting a biscuit at our table that will become a great influence to those around them? On the other hand, whom do we fail to give a biscuit to that could have led to a great miracle?

No doubt, when we move forward with our mission we will face a stir and criticism as well. In the early 1960's, our family conducted a tent revival in Pascagoula, Mississippi and people complained to the authorities about the noise that we were causing in the surrounding area. Dad faced criticism, numerous threats and complaints, but he pressed on. It got so bad that on one occasion someone tossed a pipe bomb out of a car as it passed. Fortunately, it ricocheted off one of the outer tent posts and landed in the parking area. Miraculously, it only spewed a few sparks; spun around and fizzled (could have been a burnt biscuit). In Dad's account of the situation, he declares that the Holy Spirit defused the bomb. What was intended to bring harm actually became a blessing. As a result, of the scary but miraculous event, many people gave their hearts to Jesus that night.

That is not all! The revival continued and the decision was made to build a permanent church right there. Oh my, there is more. The pastors in the area criticized dad and said if he proceeded with the plan of building a church, they would begin the process of revoking his license. Unbelievably, these were leaders within the same organization for which the church was being built. Dad, as Jesus did, refocused them on his mission. Dad had left a very lucrative job to pursue his ministry and God had performed miracles and had been faithful throughout the journey. There was no turning back. He was going to listen to the "ruler." Dad proceeded in building the church and they proceeded in revoking Dad's license. Through many more trials, tribulations, and miracles, the church was built and it still exists today. After a change of leadership in the organization, Dad's license was renewed. Apologies were made, accepted and a great church established. If you are in the Pascagoula, Mississippi area, you should visit East Side Assembly of God. When you do, you will know the barrier of criticism that was faced and overcome in order for that church to exist. Dad would be glad you came. His desire was that everybody gets a biscuit.

Too Busy

No doubt, we live in a fast-paced world and have many problems of our own. In this setting, it is easy to fail to take time to be a biscuit giver. If we are not careful, procrastination can prevail resulting in burnt biscuits in the oven or stale biscuits in the basket. Proverbs 3:28 admonishes us not to put off helping someone tomorrow, if we have the capacity to do it now. *"Do not say to your neighbor, "Come back tomorrow and I'll give it to you"—when you already have it with you."* (Prov. 3:28 NIV) Jesus gives us a further example of how we should take time to "love our neighbors as ourselves." in the parable of the Good Samaritan.

> *"In reply Jesus said: "A man was going down from Jerusalem to Jericho, when he was attacked by robbers. They stripped him of his clothes, beat him and went away, leaving him half dead. A priest happened to be going down the same road, and when he saw the man, he passed by on the other side. So too, a Levite, when he came to the place and saw him, passed by on the other side. But a Samaritan, as he traveled, came where the man was; and when he saw him, he took pity on him. He went to him and bandaged his wounds, pouring on oil and wine. Then he put the man on his own donkey, brought him to an inn and took care of him. The next day he took out two denarii and gave them to the innkeeper. 'Look after him,' he said, 'and when I return, I will reimburse you for any extra*

expense you may have.' "Which of these three do you think was a neighbor to the man who fell into the hands of robbers?" The expert in the law replied, "The one who had mercy on him." Jesus told him, "Go and do likewise."
Luke 10:30-37, NIV

In this parable, a man was beaten, robbed and left on the side of the road. Two individuals, a Priest and a Levite, passed by but did not take the time to help him. However, a Samaritan stopped and ministered to the man's need. Interestingly enough, the Samaritan was the least likely to help due to the fact there were great cultural differences between the Jews and the Samaritans. Good news here is the biscuit giving process overcame the culture barrier. Jesus instructs us to be like the Good Samaritan, helping others in times of suffering, and not like the Priest and Levite who neglected their neighbor.

Until we take time to help our neighbor, the love we say we have is only an emotion. It is when we take time to act on the need that we are fulfilling our biscuit giving responsibility. John chapter 13 verse 35 tells us, it is by the love we show, they will know we are his disciples. *"By this everyone will know that you are My disciples, if you have love and unselfish concern for one another." (*Jn. 13:35, AMP)

To be an effective biscuit giver we have to overcome the barrier of time. A good way to do that is to budget time for biscuit giving, just as we would budget money.

Imagine you had a bank account that deposited $86,400 each morning. The account carried over no balance from day to day, allowed you to keep no cash balance, and every evening canceled whatever part of the amount you had failed to use during the day. What would you do? Draw out every dollar each day!

We all have such a bank account. Its name is Time. Every morning, it credits you with 86,400 seconds. Every night it writes off, as lost, whatever time you have fail to use wisely. It carries over no balance from day to day. It allows no overdraft so you cannot borrow against yourself or use more time than you have. Each day, the account starts fresh. Each night, it destroys an unused time. If you fail to use the day's deposits, it is your loss and you cannot appeal to get it back.

There is never any borrowing time. You cannot take a loan out on your time or against someone else's. The time you have is the time you have and that is that. Time management is yours to decide how you spend the time, just as with money. It is never the case of us not having enough time to do things, but the case of whether we want to do them and where they fall in our priorities.

Personality Traits

We may feel we do not possess the right personality to be a biscuit giver and allow that to be a barrier. All of us are wired differently with various personalities, physical abilities, and mental abilities. Some are outspoken and bold, others are quiet and timid, but all of us can find a niche that suits our personality in the biscuit giving process. Some of us are comfortable speaking to large crowds, other are like "I can't do that." Some are behind the scenes workers who quietly get things done. Some are cooks, and actually cook biscuits. All of the parts work together for good. In Romans it declares, "We know that all things work together for good to them that love

God, to them who are called according to his purpose." (Rom. 8:28, NIV) Truly, we are all called to fulfill his purpose, and as we have clearly seen, his whole purpose is "biscuit giving. He gave Jesus, the bread of life, so we could have abundant life. "All things" includes whatever contribution we make from our walk of life, and unique make up.

Additionally, Ephesians 4:11, points out that there are various roles involved in the process of lifting each other up.

> *"So Christ himself gave the apostles, the prophets, the evangelists, the shepherds and teachers, to equip the saints for the work of ministry, for building up the body of Christ, until we all attain to the unity of the faith and of the knowledge of the Son of God, to mature manhood, to the measure of the stature of the fullness of Christ, so that we may no longer be children, tossed to and fro by the waves and carried about by every wind of doctrine, by human cunning, by craftiness in deceitful schemes. Rather, speaking the truth in love, we are to grow up in every way into him who is the head, into Christ, from whom the whole body, joined and held together by every joint with which it is equipped, when each part is working properly, makes the body grow so that it builds itself up in love. "*
>
> Eph. 4:11-16, ESV

Jesus explained in John 4:36, even though there are sowers and reapers, both will rejoice together. Regardless of our role in the process, each of us is equally important. We should never doubt our significance or the impact our role is in the biscuit giving process. God will use us with whatever our capacity is. We just have to be yielded vessels.

For 35 years, Kathy and I were part of our family singing group, The Gospel Four. Even though the name said Four, we actually had as many as eight including musicians. Kathy, Lois (her mom), and Chopper (her dad) were the main singers. I played bass guitar and sang a little. Additionally, we had a drummer, lead guitar, acoustic guitar, percussion accessories, and Kathy played piano as she sang. Now each one of us had our individual role, but collectively the sound was great. On some occasions when one of us could not come, there was an obvious difference and we recognized the value of everyone in the group.

Moreover, there was O.B. Loper who volunteered to drive the bus for us. He could not sing or play an instrument, but his value contributed to the group greatly. Occasionally, he could not come and we would take turns driving in his place. Wow, did we ever recognize how valuable he was. O.B. found his niche as a biscuit giver in a singing group, but could not sing, however he could drive. (More about this later)

Each of our individual roles was important, but we needed each other's contribution in order to have a great sound. I can only imagine what the sound would have been if we only had eight bass players, drummers, or altos, and so on. 1 Corinthians 12, gives a scriptural perspective of working together. *"If the whole body were an eye, where would the sense of hearing be? If the whole body were an ear, where would the sense of smell be? But in fact God has placed the parts in the body, every one of them just as he wanted them to be." (1 Cor. 12:17-18 NIV)*

All of us are a part of the body God desires to use for His purpose. He made us to be used right where we are, in the way He desires. Therefore, we just have to be who we are, do what we do and God will use it for his glory.

Chapter 21

Barriers to Biscuit Receiving

"Every good and perfect gift is from above, coming down from the Father of the heavenly lights, who does not change like shifting shadows."
James 1:17, NIV

In order for the biscuit giving cycle to be complete, receiving the biscuit must occur. The scripture in Acts 20:35, tells us that it is more blessed to give than to receive. However, when we accept the gift, the giving process is fulfilled. In essence, receiving is giving because as we accept the gift, we are giving the opportunity for the blessing to be released for the giver. Our failure to accept a gift can actually block a blessing for the giver and the receiver.

Paul indicated to the people in Philippians 4:17, they should give, not because he needed it, but rather that giving will be credited to their account. Here we see he received the gift because of the desire for them to be blessed. The biscuit giving process is cyclical. Once we receive, we give, then receive again and give again. Ecclesiastes declares, "Cast your bread on the waters, for you will find it after many days." (Eccles. 11:1, ESV) We have to receive the biscuit when it returns for "biscuit giving" to be complete. Galatians chapter 6 states, "And let us not grow weary of doing good, for in due season we will reap, if we do not give up." (Gal. 6:9, ESV) Receiving is a "good" work because it opens the door for miracles. The following pages will examine some of the barriers we can face in accepting biscuits.

Doubt

At times, we do not receive a biscuit because we doubt it is genuine. Because of allowing doubt to creep in, we miss receiving a potential blessing. Additionally, there are people who are pretending to be biscuit givers, but have deceptive motives by giving in order to get something in return. Many times, my thoughts default to suspicion of trickery when I receive a call offering me something for "free." Have you ever been selected to receive a "free gift" if you will respond to an email, or give your personal information? Swindles of this nature open the door for doubt.

In my book *These Old Shoes*, I shared this story but it bears repeating here. One time while dad was out of town preaching a revival, our family was completely out of food. Mom was crying and praying about the need. She had made a list of everything we needed to sustain us until dad returned. Not long after, a couple called and said the Lord had laid our family on their heart and impressed them to bring us some groceries. They did not ask what we needed; they just said they were bringing groceries. Of course, doubt rose up in Mom and she said, "How will they know what to bring. Oh well, if God told them to bring groceries, He can tell them what to bring." Mom put Matthew 7:7 to the test that day and God came through.

"Ask and it will be given to you; seek and you will find; knock and the door will be opened to you For everyone who asks receives; the one who seeks finds; and to the one who knocks, the door will be opened. Which of you, if your son asks for bread, will give him a stone?" (Matt. 7:7-9, NIV)

When the couple arrived with the groceries, biscuit giving overruled doubt because everything on Mom's list (and more) was in the supply they brought. I can honestly say, through all the years of financial struggles in the ministry, we never missed a meal, unless we were fasting. God always sent a "biscuit giver" just in time. God always makes a way, we should never doubt. Sometimes he sends it to us, and other times he makes an opportunity for us to earn it. *"I have been young, and now am old; yet have I not seen the righteous forsaken, nor his seed begging for bread."* (Ps. 37:25, KJV)

When I was a student in middle and high school, before the days of federally subsidized school nutrition programs, I often would not have money for lunch. However, the cafeteria manager arranged for me to get a free lunch every day in exchange for me cleaning the tables after my lunch wave. Some days I would even help wash the dishes. In addition, there were a few benefits. I really loved the big peanut butter cookies and on days when they were served, the cafeteria workers would make sure I had a good supply of leftover cookies. This situation was just a foretaste of things to come in my adult life, because God has always made a way when there seemed to be no way. *"And my God will meet all your needs according to the riches of his glory in Christ Jesus."* (Phil. 4:19, NIV)

We can be our own stream of doubt if we do not stand firm on our faith when we pray. After we pray for a particular need, we should behave as if the prayer has been answered. We should visualize what we are praying for as if it already exists. Sometimes we can talk ourselves out of believing, and into doubting what God is doing in the invisible realm. Hebrews chapter 11 declares, "Now faith is the substance of things hoped for, the evidence of things not seen." (Heb. 11:1, KJV) It is easy to doubt things that are not seen. In my own prayer life, I have included a "prayer art gallery" where I draw a picture to help me visualize the result of what I am praying for and cite a scripture that supports my request. When I am tempted to doubt and speak a negative word, I change my focus and look at the picture (my evidence of things not seen) I have drawn. By the way, I am not an artist at all, but I can draw stick figures, etc. to portray the image. Since we are talking about biscuits, this technique is my way of starving doubt, and feeding faith. The art gallery builds my faith when I reflect on the pictures of prayers that have been answered.

I have never seen mana fall from the sky, but I have seen mana revealed in the form of God's provision. Sometimes it is an opportunity to earn and reap a harvest, a good deal, or extended life expectancy on property and life. In the book of Revelation, there is reference to hidden mana that only the redeemed can see. *"Whoever has ears, let them hear what the Spirit says to the churches. To the one who is victorious, I will give some of the hidden manna. I will also give that person a white stone with a new name written on it, known only to the one who receives it."* (Rev. 2:17, NIV)

Who are the "victorious" referred to in this scripture? They are the followers of Christ who overcome the power and temptation of this world and hold fast, without doubt, to faith in Christ until the end. The "victorious" demonstrates complete reliance upon Jesus through it all. The hidden mana is ours, therefore, we must not doubt. Through our faith, we will be sustained. Most importantly, Jesus, the manna from heaven is coming soon and only the redeemed will see him.

Sympathy

When we are biscuit "givers", it is easy to overlook the need to be biscuit "receivers" from those less fortunate than us. However, as noted earlier, the giving process is not complete until someone receives. John 12 indicates, "For the poor you will always have with you, but you do not always have me." (Jn. 12:8, ESV) This is not a pass to say, "Oh well that is just the way it is." Interestingly, it is the opposite because the intent here is to compel us to open our hands wide because it is an ongoing fact of life. However, being less fortunate should not preclude anyone from getting in on the biscuit giving process. How else will they overcome being less fortunate? As they give, the process begins and blessings head their way. Proverbs reminds us that the "The rich and poor have this in common, the Lord is the maker of them all." (Prov. 22:2, NKJV) Therefore, the same principals of giving apply to rich and the poor.

I have been so blessed, that many times it is difficult to accept gifts especially when I know the person giving is in need themselves. I have learned to accept the gifts because by allowing them to give, I have given them the opportunity to open the floodgate of blessing on their lives.

Earlier we shared the account of the widow who gave all she had which was the equivalent of 2 pennies. Jesus noted that others had given from their wealth, but she had given all she had. The gift was accepted even though it must have been difficult to do so. Additionally, this same principal applies in the word of Paul when he told his audience that they should give, not because he needed the gift, but they needed to give in order to participate in the giving and receiving process.

I remember as a young child, while dad was a tent evangelist; many times, we were ministering in rural areas. In some cases, the residents did not have a great deal of money and instead of bringing money; they would have what they called a "pounding." When the pastor first announced to come prepared to give the Amacker Family a "pounding" tonight, I was concerned. A "pounding" sounded serious! What were they going to "pound" us with? Is it going to hurt? After all, I thought Dad had preached good messages and we did not deserve a "pounding!" I learned later, with much relief, that a "pounding" was the practice of people bringing food from their garden and other items to benefit people in the church. One time a man brought chicken. The only problem was—it was a live chicken. I do not remember the result of the chicken, but I am certain it was not pretty. Nonetheless, we were very appreciative of their contributions and recognized they were bringing what they had. God always supplied our need through their giving, and I know, because of their giving, He met theirs too. It is a process and sometimes it is more blessed to receive than to give.

Lack of Acceptance of the Giver

In what circumstances, are we allowed to reject a gift? What happens when someone rejects a sacrifice, a gift or offering? Can we just say no thanks? Sometimes, we choose to refuse to accept help because we do not like the person or organization that is giving. In some cases, we do not accept the gift if it goes against our purpose and core values. Here are some notable Biblical examples of rejecting gifts.

Elisha turned down Naaman's gift. After Naaman was healed, he presented Elisha with a large gift, but Elisha rejected it. In this case, Elisha was aware that the gift of healing came from God not himself. He did not want to accept the gift for himself in honor of Almighty God. Additionally, God himself rejected an offering from Cain. The reason for God rejecting the gift is not known.

In the story of Esau and Jacob, Esau gave up his birthright to Jacob in exchange for a bowl of soup. When they grew older, Jacob with the help of his mother Rebekah tricked Isaac, his father, into blessing Jacob, instead of his older brother, Esau. When Esau learned of this plot, he then swore he would kill his brother after their father died. Jacob fled again, with help from his mother. Through the years Jacob prospered, though, at God's instruction, he returned to the land of his birth, where he confronted his brother, Esau. We must remember that Jacob was a biscuit "taker" in this chain of events and his part of the reconciliation was vital.

Jacob was fearful that Esau would carry out his promise to kill him and sent a series of peace offerings to Esau including hundreds of goats, sheep, camels, cows, bulls and donkeys. The next morning, Jacob (new name Israel) met his brother. Before greeting him, Israel bowed seven times. Esau embraced him, and they both wept. What happened next was a classic biscuit giving moment.

Esau initially did not accept the gifts, though Jacob and or Israel insisted and he eventually accepted the gifts. Therefore, Jacob received the gift of peace from God when Esau accepted the gift. If Esau had not accepted the gift, one wonders if the reconciliation would have been complete and peace granted. If Esau had persisted in his discord with Jacob, the process would not have worked.

We have to remove the barrier of unforgiveness. If there is a situation between an individual and us that is causing the rejection of a gift, we must address it through confrontation and forgiveness. As in the case with Jacob and Esau, peace will not come until reconciliation is made.

We can miss God's blessings if we allow barriers to block us from receiving gifts. When Kathy and I were just beginning our family, a gentleman kept asking to arrange a time with us to discuss financial planning. We kept putting him off, partly because of our personal differences. He was persistent and I finally agreed to a meeting. As I listened to what he had to say, I realized he was exactly right and made the changes he was recommending. I can say, after following through with that plan for the next 40 years, change he brought to us benefited us tremendously, even to this day. Kathy and I almost rejected a blessing from God because of the messenger. Further, we are friends to this day with the man we once avoided. I thank him every time I see him and let him know it is still working.

Rejecting a biscuit can be hurtful to the person being rejected and to the one doing the rejecting. Jesus hurts when we do not accept his gift to us. By laying down his life, he offers to us the gift of eternal life. When we reject His gift, it is hurtful to Him, and devastating to us. *"For what shall it profit a man, if he shall gain the whole world, and lose his own soul?"* (Mark 8:36, KJV)

Martha Effect

Have you ever been guilty of devoting so much time and effort to a project that you do not take time to receive a biscuit? If we only give and never receive, inevitably burnout will occur. There has to be a season for receiving. Ecclesiastes Chapter 3 declares there is a season for everything. We have to recognize what season we are in and respond appropriately.

> *"To everything there is a season, and a time to every purpose under the heaven: A time to be born, and a time to die; a time to plant, and a time to pluck up that which is planted; A time to kill, and a time to heal; a time to break down, and a time to build up; A time to weep, and a time to laugh; a time to mourn, and a time to dance; A time to cast away stones, and a time to gather stones together; a time to embrace, and a time to refrain from embracing; A time to get, and a time to lose; a time to keep, and a time to cast away; A time to rend, and a time to sew; a time to keep silence, and a time to speak; A time to love, and a time to hate; a time of war, and a time of peace."*
> Eccles. 3:1-8, KJV

The story of Martha preparing a meal for a special gathering at her house with Jesus is a vivid example of recognizing the season in which one may find themselves. This story is recounted in Luke 10:38-42 and John 12:2, which involves Mary and Martha, sisters of Lazarus. Martha was busy preparing a meal for Jesus and the disciples, but Mary was sitting at the feet of Jesus listening and worshiping him. Martha was perturbed and asked Jesus to scold Mary because she was doing all the work while Mary was only sitting at the feet of Jesus. Jesus indicated to her that Mary actually had her priorities right.

We too, at times can allow our busy lives of service distract us from spending time with Jesus and listening to his word. A "Barryism" here is what I call the "Martha Effect." Jesus admonished Martha for being worried and upset about all of the details and not for serving. Service is a good thing, but sitting at Jesus' feet is best. We must remember in what season we are living. *'But the Lord said to her, "My dear Martha, you are worried and upset over all these details! There is only one thing worth being concerned about. Mary has discovered it, and it will not be taken away from her."'* (Luke 10: 41-42, NLT)

I have been guilty of this very thing. Serving as minister of music, parallel with my education career for 47 years, led me into the "Martha Effect" many times. After working all week at school, and preparing music for Sunday's church service, I found myself busy. On Sunday mornings, we would arrive early, rehearse with the praise team, set things up for the choir, do sound checks for special music, and sometimes teach a Sunday school class. Then I led praise and worship, directed the choir, and participated in the preliminaries for the service. When it was all done and I was seated, at God's table, I was too tired to receive my biscuit. I am sure I missed some valuable points of important messages along the way due to the "Martha Effect." I would like to stress here the importance of our daily personal devotion time. We cannot just rely on our worship time at church alone to be enough. We must find the time to sit at Jesus' feet and receive the biscuit He has come to give.

Lack of Understanding

Sometimes we reject biscuits because of a lack of understanding, preconceived notions, or beliefs that we do not like something that is actually good. Sometimes we just do not recognize God is moving on our behalf, in his time and in his way. *"Trust in the LORD with all thine heart; and lean not unto thine own understanding. In all thy ways acknowledge him, and he shall direct thy paths."* (Prov. 3:5-6, KJV)

In the second book of Kings chapter 3, the Israelites faced a battle with Moab and were fearful of being defeated. Through the prophet Elisha, God told the people he was about to bless them, even though they would not see it coming. He told them to get ready! *"You will see neither wind nor rain, says the LORD, but this valley will be filled with water. You will have plenty for yourselves and your cattle and other animals. But this is only a simple thing for the LORD, for he will make you victorious over the army of Moab!"* (2 Kings 3:17-18, NLT)

God instructed the Israelites to dig ditches to contain the blessing that was coming. He indicated they would not see the rain or the wind, but He would fill the ditches and the valley with more water than they would need. Further, He informed them that He would deliver Moab into their hands.

Whether we see it or not, understand it or not, God is moving on our behalf. We cannot become impatient or fearful just dig the ditches. The story is told that, a man walked to the top of a hill to talk to God. The man asked, "God, what's a million years to you?" God said, "A minute." Then the man asked, "Well, what's a million dollars to you?" God said, "A penny." Then the man asked, "God, can I have a penny?" God said, "Sure, in a minute."

I do not know about you but I will take God's blessing in His time. If it is a penny in a minute, it is enough. Waiting on God is not wasting time. Sometimes a blessing does not look like a blessing and we resist it. I remember resisting my parents when they insisted I eat something unfamiliar to me. Often when this happened, after eating it, I discovered it was actually good.

As mentioned earlier, Kathy spent the last few years of her career as an intervention teacher at Ocean Springs High School. Many of her students were English as Second Language (ESL) students from other countries and she had a great relationship with them. As most teachers do, she had a few little tricks to keep the students engaged. In this case, it was a stash of candy, chips, and an assortment of junk food (junk biscuits) she would offer the kids occasionally. One student from China declined to accept the candy when he first joined the class. He said, "We do not eat junk food in China." Kathy and the other students were surprised, but accepted his answer (and they ate ALL of the candy). Well, as time passed, the student from China began nibbling a little bit on some of the candy and before long; he was all in on the candy thing. He said, "Mrs. Amacker, where is the candy? I like it now." Everyone was amused at his change of heart about the junk food.

Lack of understanding or things that may be contrary to which we are accustomed can compel us to reject a biscuit. We are living in an age where knowledge and information abound. It seems every day a new study is released that changes concepts we believed in the past. With the advancement of technology and research development, we discover everyday things we once believed may not have been true and other things we did not realize until now became known. Not to say we were deceived, rather over time we have learned more. We have to be more receptive and adaptable to new information and receive the biscuit of knowledge.

I believe this is true in a spiritual sense too. Hold on! I am not suggesting God has changed. However, I believe we are understanding prophecy more clearly now than in the past. Daniel gives us that reason. *"But you, Daniel, roll up and seal the words of the scroll until the time of the end. Many will go here and there to increase knowledge."* (Dan. 12:4, NIV)

This passage was given to Daniel in a vision pertaining to the end times. He is told to seal this information until the time of the end. The "time of the end" was further described as a time when people will go back and forth, and knowledge will increase. No doubt, over the past few decades, travel and information have exploded. With that passage in mind, one cannot help but think we are in the "time of the end" and the seal placed on that information has been lifted.

A fresh biscuit of knowledge is coming our way and we have to be prepared to receive it. Now that the seal is gone and prophecy is being fulfilled, we do not have to speculate about meanings that may have been misunderstood in the past. Things are becoming more and more abundantly clear. It is time for the church to look past traditional denominational boundaries and see the bigger picture through the lifted seal.

Be forewarned! Satan is in the deceiving business and we will have to have our spiritual capacity fully engaged to sort it all out. Not every biscuit in the basket may contain ingredients of the bread of life, which should be rejected.

The Psalmist invites us all to, "Taste and see that the Lord is good." He says, "Oh, taste and see that the LORD is good! Blessed is the man who takes refuge in him". (Ps. 34:8, ESV) This verse begins with an invitation to draw close to God and experience his goodness. Then it declares we can take refuge in him. He is there with us in the good times and the bad times. He offers us everything we need in this life and everlasting life. He is a biscuit giver and everybody gets a biscuit at his table.

Pride

At times, pride can hinder us from accepting biscuits. We have to admit needing something in order to receive it. Everybody needs help in one way or another occasionally. Sometimes our basket is empty and we need a refill. In these times, the biscuit giving process is powerful. When the opportunity arises for one person to be a biscuit giver and another to be a biscuit receiver, a biscuit giving moment occurs. I have heard it said, "If you see a turtle sitting on top of a fence post, rest assured it had help getting there" and that is perfectly fine.

We can be too proud to go through the receiving process. Remember, Naaman almost missed his healing because he was offended that Elisha did not come out to greet him. Instead, he sent his servant. After all, Naaman was a "mighty captain." Additionally, he was upset by being required to dip seven times in the muddy Jordan River in order to receive his miracle. He noted there were clearer rivers back home. Fortunately, he overcame pride, accepted the biscuit, and he was healed.

Sometimes we may be too proud to admit we do not know nor how to do something and will not receive help from others who do know. One of the greatest gifts one can receive is that of instruction from a wise person. The book of Proverbs declares, *"Hear instruction and be wise, and do not neglect it."* (Prov. 8:33, ESV)

There have been times when I neglected instruction from a wise person and regretted it (I did not dip in the Jordan). Unfortunately, this tendency is inherent in human nature.

On one trip to Disney World in Orlando, Florida, with our children, I was riding with our son Bradley, on the Frog ride. On this ride you drive (sort of) the frog car through a maze. Well, Bradley, who was about four years old at the time, insisted on driving the frog. I had my reservations, but gave in and let him try. Oh my! We had a bumpy ride bouncing from side to side. We pressed on, until the track took us into a dark tunnel and suddenly coming toward us from the opposite direction was a bright light with a loud train whistle. As it got closer and closer, Bradley bailed. He said, "Here daddy, YOU DRIVE!" We made it safely through the rest of the ride and Bradley was very appreciative. This episode reveals how quickly situations can turn to disasters if we fail to heed advice from those more experienced than we are.

(Back to the turtle) When we do receive help, a humble "Thank You," goes a long way. Once we receive help and are feeling high and lifted up while sitting on the fence, we have to remember we had help getting there and will need help getting down. There is no need for that turtle (or us) to sit on that post looking like he got there by himself. Everybody knows he had help. If we are not careful, we can be like that silly turtle and miss the blessing of giving a biscuit of encouragement to those who helped us.

Low Self Esteem

Another barrier to accepting a biscuit is that of not feeling worthy to be the recipient. The fact of the matter is who you are, where you live, who your parents are and when you are born does matter in our society today. Malcolm Gladwell quantifies this notion in his book Outliers (2008, Little, Brown and Company). His data supports the theory that one's success academically, athletically and professionally can be determined by his or her birthdate, birthplace, and background. If you happen to fall within the less advantageous range of one of those categories, it can result in low self-esteem, a feeling of unworthiness and poor performance.

One of Satan's most useful tactics is to make us feel we are too bad to be any good. He will continually point out our failures, disappointments and shortcomings in order to make us feel as though we are not worthy to receive biscuits. He would have us believe we are too far gone to accept the bread of life. However, Jesus offers the biscuit of everlasting life to everyone. *"For whosoever shall call upon the name of the Lord shall be saved."* (Rom. 10:13, KJV)

Satan is the one who tries to make us feel unworthy. He is the accuser of the brethren. Keep in mind he is not our accuser before God, but before others. His strategy is to slander us to our peers. If that does not work he slanders us to ourselves. As biscuit givers and receivers, we have to be keen to his plots and deflect them. As a biscuit giver, we should not be caught up in being a part of tearing down others around us, and finding fault with each other. This practice prevents us from working together and being effective biscuit givers or receivers.

As a biscuit receiver, we have to accept encouragement, especially the fact that God loves us and we ARE worthy. Satan would love us to reject the bread of life and live under the feeling of condemnation. The Holy Spirit does not bring condemnation, but brings conviction, which is a work of love. In

Romans 7, Paul reveals his own human frailty. He says, "I do not do what I want to do, and I do what I do not want to do. I desire to do well, but I do not. He later gives all of us hope in our own human frailty. "The answer is in Jesus Christ our Lord." *"Oh, what a miserable person I am! Who will free me from this life that is dominated by sin and death? Thank God! The answer is in Jesus Christ our Lord. So you see how it is: In my mind I really want to obey God's law, but because of my sinful nature I am a slave to sin."* (Rom. 7:24-25, NLT)

No matter what we go through, where or when we are born, we have value. A popular speaker started off a seminar by holding up a $20 bill. A crowd of 200 had gathered to hear him speak. He asked, "Who would like this $20 bill?" All 200 hands went up. He said, "I am going to give this $20 to one of you but first, let me do this." He crumpled the up bill. He then asked, "Who still wants it?" All 200 hands were still raised. "Well," he replied, "What if I do this?" Then he dropped the bill on the ground and stomped on it with his shoes. He picked it up, and showed it to the crowd. The bill was all crumpled and dirty. "Now who still wants it?" All the hands still went up. This demonstration gives insight to the fact that no matter what was done to the money, it did not decrease in value. It was still worth $20. Likewise, in our lives, circumstances may crumple and grind us into the dirt, but no matter what happens, or what will happen, we will never lose our value. God still wants us and His hand still goes up for us no matter where we are.

During difficult times, consider that God is working His plan. His strategy may be strange to us, but we have to trust Him. Jesus, the King of Kings was worthy of the most extravagant accommodations, but was born in a poor lowly stable. This strategy confused Satan. Herod was looking in the wrong place for Jesus. He never considered, from what he had heard, that Jesus would be born in a stable. Similarly, in the case of Moses, God's strategy confused Satan. When Moses was sent down the Nile River, it confused Satan. He could not find him. In both incidences, God had greater plans to be fulfilled in the near future. The same is true for us because our current circumstance is not the end of the story. In fact, Satan cannot get to us either because we are covered by Jesus' blood shed at Calvary. In due time, God's plan is fulfilled and our true value is revealed. You are special! Never forget it!

In Dad's pastoring ministry when my brother and I were young, we participated in the praise and worship service by playing the tambourine and maracas. We would switch instruments every other service. If I played the maracas one service, I would switch to tambourine and my brother would go to maracas the next service. One night when it was time for service, I could not find the tambourine and could not play. Dad noticed that I had not played and asked why. When I told Dad I could not find the tambourine, he inquired and discovered that the music director had hidden it. Dad asked him why and he told Dad, "Barry is the worst tambourine player in the history of tambourine playing." This did not sit well with Dad. At the next service, Dad got with my brother and me before the music started and showed us a stash of about 10 tambourines he had hidden in his office. He said, "If anytime in the future we could not find a tambourine to play for the service, grab one of these."

I may have been the worst tambourine player in the world at that time, but I had jumped in to give it my best, and I was learning. Well the rest of the story is that, I grew up to be a musician and earned a full music scholarship to the University of South Alabama. I became a band director, Teacher of the Year for Mobile County School District, a church music director and Superintendent of the Year for the state of Mississippi. We never know what God is trying to do through others and us. We have to be patient and press on. The "hidden tambourine" episode stuck with me and as I developed young musicians in school and church, I was always sensitive to allow space for the musicians to grow into what God was planning for them.

God desires to use us according to the capabilities He has given us. We all have our unique genetic potential in our physical, mental, emotional, and spiritual makeup. Our responsibility is to be the best we can be, without trying to be as good as someone else is. There may be times when our genetic potential does not seem to be sufficient, but God will use us and make up the difference.

This little story gives a good illustration of using our genetic potential appropriately.

> *A mother and a baby camel were lying around under a tree. Then the baby camel asked, "Why do camels have humps?" The mother camel considered this and said, "We are desert animals so we have the humps to store water so we can survive with very little water." The baby camel thought for a moment then said, "Ok, why, are our legs long and our feet rounded?" The mama replied, "They are meant for walking in the desert." The baby paused. After a beat, the camel asked, "Why are our eyelashes long? Sometimes they get in my way." The mama responded, "Those long thick eyelashes protect*

your eyes from the desert sand when it blows in the wind. The baby thought and thought. Then he said, "I see. So, the hump is to store water when we are in the desert, the legs are for walking through the desert and these eye lashes protect my eyes from the desert then why in the Zoo?"

Indeed, God has given us what we need to fulfill our intended purpose, but it is worthless if we are in the wrong place, at the wrong time and not using what we have.

I was amazed while at the gym the other day as I witnessed a young woman who was so positive and energetic with her workout. After closer observation, I noticed her arm was much shorter than the other was and her hand on the shorter arm was not positioned correctly. She did not let this stop her workout. She had found ways to compensate for the lack of use of one arm. She inspired me so much (I received a biscuit of inspiration from her) with her attitude, work ethic and pressonabilitly (Barryism).

There are many examples in the Bible when the underdog was victorious. In one battle, David's army was facing a strong opponent. He was big and strong. Amazingly, genetics had given him six toes, and six fingers on each foot and hand. Despite the odds, God gave the victory. *"In still another battle, which took place at Gath, there was a huge man with six fingers on each hand and six toes on each foot—twenty-four in all. He also was descended from Rapha. When he taunted Israel, Jonathan son of Shimeah, David's brother, killed him."* (2 Sam. 21:20-21, NIV)

In our daily lives, we have to allow God the opportunity to give the biscuit of His power to intervene for our shortcomings. If we sit back with the feeling, we are not good enough, the biscuit falls by the wayside. No matter what the odds appear to be, Press on!

Rebellion

Of all the barriers to receiving biscuits, rebellion is the most consequential. The Biblical definition of rebellion is described as an attitude displayed to contradict authority. Rebellion started from the beginning of Creation. When God created Adam and Eve, He put them in the Garden of Eden, and gave them instructions regarding what to do and not to do. He had given the biscuit of the ages, though they rebelled through disobedience.

When a Sunday school teacher asked a class of kindergarten students what was the first commandment, the response was. "The first commandment was when Eve told Adam to eat the apple." Of course, that is not the first commandment, but it does have significance. This act of rebellion had an impact on God's plan for all mankind.

Rebellion is still alive and well in our world today. After God moved to plan B to redeem us through Jesus Christ, many continue to rebel by rejecting the word of God. We know that Jesus and the Word are one in the same. John declares, *"In the beginning was the Word, and the Word was with God, and the Word was God."* (Jn. 1:1, NIV) Jesus proclaimed to the people that He was the Bread of Life that came down from heaven and whoever would come to him will not go hungry or thirsty.

"Then Jesus declared, "I am the bread of life. Whoever comes to me will never go hungry, and whoever believes in me will never be thirsty. I am the bread of life. Your ancestors ate the manna in the wilderness, yet they died. But here is the bread that comes down from heaven, which anyone may eat and not die. I am the living bread that came down from heaven. Whoever eats this bread will live forever. This bread is my flesh, which I give for the life of the world."
Jn. 6:35, 48-51, NIV

In Revelation Chapter 10, we see John, the revelator, actually eats the word. The angel instructed John to eat the "little book." As far as it can be determined, "the little book" is the word of God. The angel told John that when he ate the book it would be bitter in his stomach but sweet in his mouth. John ate the book and it was as the angel said. This act is incredible! John accepted the biscuit of the ages that was brought by the angel. Yes, it was the Word and Jesus is the word. Jesus made it clear that he is the bread of life, "the little book" if you will. Yet, due to rebellion, many people do not partake, by rejecting the word.

Hold on! Before jumping on "those bad" sinners who reject the word, we need to dive deeper. Those who have accepted Jesus and who are Christians can also be guilty of rejecting the biscuit. John found the little book to be sweet in his mouth, but bitter in his stomach. When we first become Christians, we are excited and how sweet it is to be born again. All things are new and our sins have been washed away, thank you Jesus. Nevertheless, as we begin to digest the word, God challenges us to grow. We have to get off the milk, and get a taste of the meat (a steak biscuit) of the word. Many do not take growth seriously. Paul, in 1 Corinthians, expresses his concern on the growth of the spiritual growth of the early Christians. *"I had to feed you with milk, not with solid food, because you weren't ready for anything stronger. And you still aren't ready."* (1 Cor. 3:2, NLT)

    God intends for everyone to get a biscuit. Whether we are a new Christian, or a longtime believer we should never rebel against his instruction. His word is there for all of us to learn and grow to our full spiritual potential. The biscuits he gives are nourishing to our souls.

SECTION 4

Setting the Table

~~~·~~~

> *"Come, all you who are thirsty, come to the waters; and you who have no money, come, buy and eat! Come, buy wine and milk without money and without cost. Why spend money on what is not bread, and your labor on what does not satisfy? Listen, listen to me, and eat what is good, and you will delight in the richest of fare. Give ear and come to me; listen, that you may live. I will make an everlasting covenant with you, my faithful love promised to David."*
> <p align="right">Isa. 55:1-3, NIV</p>

In this scripture, God, the original biscuit giver gives a broad and all-encompassing invitation. He sends the invitation to the thirsty, to those without money, to those with money, to those who are discouraged and those who are confident. Honestly, this represents all of us. He offers us water, milk and wine that collectively correspond with every need we have. He offers water to refresh us, milk for nutrition and wine for an eternal jubilant life.

The table is set for everyone, with everything we need. God has done his part and it is now our turn to respond. Will we accept the biscuits? Will we transfer this gift to others by offering them biscuits?

Indeed, we should pull up a chair to the table that is spread and participate in the everlasting covenant God has promised.

Chapter 22

Communion

~~~

Earlier I referred to Revelation Chapter 10 where John actually ate the word. In a sense, we too can eat the "little book" as remembrance, through communion, of what Jesus did for us at Calvary. The most significant biscuit-giving act is when Jesus gave his life on the cross for our sins. Remembrance of this event is done through partaking of communion. Communion is done at various times within churches. Some churches do it occasionally, and others do it in every service. Sometimes families do it at home, or weddings and funerals. In fact, recently I found a CD recording of one of Dad's services where he led the church in communion. Kathy and I will actually take communion at home with Dad, who has passed away, occasionally. It is a very special time. However, no matter when or where it is done, it should be a deeply meaningful act of remembering Jesus' death and resurrection.

In the upper room, Jesus broke bread with His disciples and established a special way for them to remember His death and resurrection. A model for us to follow is found in in the New Testament.

> *"For I received from the Lord what I also passed on to you: On the night when He was betrayed, the Lord Jesus took bread, gave thanks, broke it, and said, 'This is My body, which is for you. Do this in remembrance of Me.' In the same way, after supper, He also took the cup and said, 'This cup is the new covenant established by My blood. Do this, as often as you drink it, in remembrance of Me.' For as often as you eat this bread and drink the cup, you proclaim the Lord's death until He comes."*
> 1 Cor. 11:24-26, ESV

Specifically, a cup with either wine or grape juice and either wafers or unleavened bread is used in the communion service. The bread used for communion signifies the body of Jesus, which was broken for us. He took on all sin, iniquity, rebellion, disease, grief and shame. The wine (or grape juice) represents His blood, which was shed to bring forgiveness for our sins.

At Calvary, Jesus covered our whole being encompassing our physical, mental, emotional and spiritual dimensions. When we pray over our sin (spiritual), iniquity (spiritual), rebellion (mental, emotional), disease (physical) grief (emotional) and shame (emotional/mental) we are to remember Christ's broken body and shed blood. God calls us to partake in communion with a heart that is repentant and a spirit that desires to be right with Him in all areas of our lives. *"Let a person examine himself, then, and so eat of the bread and drink of the cup."* (1 Cor. 11:28, ESV)

Our obedience in following the instruction to partake in communion with "remembrance" should involve remembering with our whole being. Physical (gut brain), mental (head brain) emotional (heart brain) and spiritual (All 3) remembrance brings us into full acceptance and application of communion for our lives. This does not mean we have to be perfect, but we have to be humble, repentant, and accept the biscuit without rebellion. If we fail to remember in this way, we are just eating crackers and drinking grape juice.

Chapter 23

Final Invitation

Jesus desires that everybody "gets a biscuit" at His table. He desires that no one should perish but have everlasting life. God sent the bread of life, Jesus Christ, that we all may be saved. *"For God so loved the world, that he gave his only begotten Son, that whosoever believeth in him should not perish, but have everlasting life."* (Jn. 3:16, KJV)

Revelation chapter 22, offers the final invitation in the scriptures to accept from the biscuit giver. *"And the Spirit and the bride say, Come. And let him that heareth say, Come. And let him that is athirst come. And whosoever will, let him take the water of life freely."* (Rev. 22:17, KJV) Jesus came as the bread of life and throughout the Bible offered himself to us. Additionally, this scripture says "And all who hear say, Come," reminding us to be biscuit givers as well by offering the invitation to others. This message is given by the Spirit and the bride "And let him who thirsts come. And whosoever desires, let him take the water of life freely." What is your response? Will you accept the bread of life? Will you answer the call to, Come? Will you accept the responsibility given as a believer to invite others to come?

On Wednesday, January 19, 1995, my daughter and I visited my Dad in the hospital where he was being cared for following a heart attack. We were very encouraged that he was doing better and cutting up in his usual way. While we were there, his lunch was brought in. Alisa thought it would be fun to feed him the way he used to feed her when she was a little girl. She even did the little airplane move and said, "Open wide, is it good?" Dad played along, but when she asked, "Is it good?" His reply was one we will never forget, he said, "No, it is not good and the only reason I am eating it is because my granddaughter is feeding it to me."

We had a delightful afternoon with Dad until it was time for us to leave for church. When we told Dad, it was time for us to leave to go to church, he responded, "Indeed, you need to go because you do not want to be late for church." Little did I know those would be his last words to me on this earth. The next day, I received the call that Dad had passed away. I was shocked and heart broken. Dad's last words to me were an invitation to church. Dad was a biscuit receiver, biscuit giver, and inviter of others to, "Come." I fondly remember in our church where he was pastor, not many services went by that we did not sing the song "Come and Dine." I can hear it now. Dad singing, Mom playing the organ and me and my older brother playing tambourine (If I could find it) and maracas. Take a minute and join right in, the lyrics are listed below:

Come and Dine
Charles B. Widmeyer, 1907

Final Invitation

Jesus has a table spread
Where the saints of God are fed,
He invites His chosen people, "Come and dine";
With his manna He doth feed
And supplies our every need:
Oh, tis sweet to sup with Jesus all the time!

Refrain
"Come and dine," the Master calleth, "Come and Dine";
You may feast at Jesus table all the time;
He who fed the multitude, turned the water into wine,
To the hungry calleth now, "Come and Dine."

The disciples came to land,
Thus obeying Christ's command,
For the Master called unto them, "Come and dine";
There they found their heart's desire,
Bread and fish upon the fire;
Thus He satisfies the hungry every time.

Soon the Lamb will take His bride
To be ever at His side,
All the host of heaven will assembled be;
Oh, 'twill be a glorious sight,
All the saints in spotless white;
And with Jesus they feast eternally

CONCLUSION

Reflecting on the biscuit giving acts presented in this book, it is apparent that miracles followed biscuit giving moments. My question is, what miracles await for God to do through us, or for us? Are we next to give, or receive a biscuit? God has already laid out the good works for us to do in advance. They are there! What are we waiting for? *"For we are God's handiwork, created in Christ Jesus to do good works, which God has prepared in advance for us to do."* (Eph. 2:10, NIV) Therefore, it is our obligation to find those opportunities, prepare ourselves and act to fulfill them. Miracles are awaiting our action.

- What if, Pat had not been making sure that everybody got a biscuit at her tables?
- What if I had said, "No thanks I don't need a biscuit with all of this food?"
- What if Naaman's wife's servant had not had the courage to speak up and stand in the gap?
- What if, Naaman had not listened to the servant girl, who was acting out of her scope of work?
- What if, Elijah had accepted the widow's resistance to what he was telling her to do, or, if she had not followed through as instructed?

- What if, Dorcas had not ministered to the women in need of clothes?
- What if, Peter was too busy to heal Dorcas?
- What if Sandra had not encouraged Andrae to finish the song?
- What if, Dad said to Alisa, "No I'm not hungry and this food is terrible?"
- What if, I had told the injured student. "No, I can't pray at school?"
- What, if the numerous biscuit givers mentioned in this book had not responded?
- What if, we tell Jesus, "No thanks?"
- What if we do not respond to opportunities already laid out before us?

The biscuit giving process is a journey and we have to start somewhere. As mentioned earlier, Kathy and I were in a gospel-singing group with her family, The Gospel Four. We traveled all over the country and ministered to multitudes of people over the years. It was quite a journey. The favorite part of the journey over the years was singing at homecomings with "dinner on the grounds" on Sundays after the morning service. Believe me, we ate many wonderful meals at these services and met many biscuit givers, literally.

On one occasion, we were scheduled to sing for a homecoming service in a place called Buzzard's Roost. This was before the days of GPS and navigation apps and we lost our way. We traveled in a big bus and maneuvering around was a chore. We stopped at a service station to ask for directions to the church. The response from the attendant was, "I know where that is, but you can't get there from here!" Our bus driver, O. B. Loper (a biscuit giver himself, because he volunteered to drive for the group) was confused and asked the attendant again for directions. The attendant again said, "You can't get there from here, but if you go up to the stop sign and go down that dirt road it will take you there." Off we went and it was a long, dusty and winding road. Along the way, we wondered if we would ever get there. Further, we wondered if anyone would attend in this very remote location. In the back of my mind was the words, "you can't get there from here" and I was beginning to believe it.

We finally arrived and to our surprise, there were hundreds of people there with cars that lined the dusty road for as far as I could see. We had a wonderful concert and the dinner on the grounds was one to remember. This was biscuit giving at its best! Along with the hundreds of people, there were many tables filled with food, desserts, sweet tea, and "stuff!" If you have read my book Power to Press On, you know the story of how I got up to weigh 190 pounds. This day was a great contributor to that condition.

Consequently, when you start to take the biscuit giving journey rest assured there will be some dusty, difficult roads and you may feel as though "you can't get there from here." Good news! No matter where you are if the journey takes you to the cross of Calvary, you can get to your destination from there. Indeed, you will get there and you will be surprised at what miracles await.

Biscuit Giver:
"Everybody Gets a Biscuit at My Table"

Dr. Barry Amacker and Pat Ellzey at Mother's Restaurant

Other Books by Dr. Barry Amacker

These Old Shoes

Shoes hold a valuable place in the physical world, but they always infer a deeper meaning. Within the pages of ***These Old Shoes,*** Barry Amacker, the author shares as a young child he offered the shoes on his feet to a boy who had none, at the time he did not realize that by removing his shoes to give someone else he would be putting on the shoes the Lord had intended for him to wear. This book also presents the idea of individuals putting on their spiritual shoes for their walk with the Lord.

"A solider without adequate footwear to provide a solid sure step will not be very effective in the heat of battle," states the author. "Similarly, we require an assortment of spiritual footwear if we are to walk firmly in the path of a victorious Christian life. As you read this book, please examine yourself and let God direct the next steps you should take the shoes you should put on."

Power to Press On

Power to Press On provides readers with practical ideas to develop physically, mentally, emotionally and spiritually. Dr.

Amacker points out to readers that in order to receive God's unlimited power, they must prepare themselves physically, mentally, emotionally, and spiritually to be a vessel God can actually use.

Power to Press On gives readers hope and a process to find their synergetic state if they are willing to be consistent in pursuing daily activities to develop in each of the physical, mental, emotional and spiritual dimensions," states Dr. Amacker. "Just like electricity, God's power is flowing, but we have to flip the switch for it to be released."

Clink

Clink: Freedom from the Chains by Dr. Barry Amacker is a powerful look at fifteen chains that hold us captive in life and prevent us from reaching our God-given potential. Dr. Amacker shows how we can use the Word of God to find freedom and purpose, and how through Him, each chain can be broken. This motivational book combines Scripture, personal anecdotes, and opportunities for reflection that will challenge and encourage readers to take hold of the chains in their own lives and break free into the life God has for them.